creative ESSENTIALS

ALSO BY CHARLES HARRIS

Police Slang
Teach Yourself: Complete Screenwriting Course

CHARLES HARRIS

JAWS IN SPACE
POWERFUL PITCHING FOR FILM AND TV SCRIPTWRITERS

creative ESSENTIALS

First published in 2016 by Kamera Books
an imprint of Oldcastle Books,
PO Box 394, Harpenden, Herts, AL5 1XJ
www.kamerabooks.com

ISBN
978-1-84344-733-7   (Print)
978-1-84344-734-4   (epub)
978-1-84344-735-1   (kindle)
978-1-84344-736-8   (pdf)

2 4 6 8 10 9 7 5 3 1

Typeset by Elsa Mathern in Franklin Gothic 9 pt
Printed and bound by CPI Group (UK) Ltd, Croydon, CR0 4YY

To everyone I've pitched to

ACKNOWLEDGEMENTS

This book builds on the chapters on developing your premise and marketing your script in my book *Teach Yourself: Complete Screenwriting Course* and I'm very grateful to Jonathan Shipley and John Murray Learning for their permission to use those parts which overlap.

Many people have contributed to this book as I learned my craft over the years, far more than I can mention here. But I do specifically want to thank Phil O'Shea, Shelley Katz, Anita Lewton, Naz Sadoughi, Paul Mendelson, Eve Richings and Ulrike Kubatta for sharing their experiences. Karol Griffiths for her support. My colleagues at Euroscript and the participants of my pitching workshops around the world, who have helped make this book what it is through their intelligent questioning and professionalism. My gratitude also goes to my agent, Julian Friedmann, his contracts manager, Resham Naqvi, as well as Ion Mills and Hannah Patterson of Kamera Books for asking me to write this in the first place.

Most importantly of all, I must thank my wife, Elaine, for her patience when faced so often by my closed study door over the last months, along with our cats, Chloe and Sasha, who are the only ones who can persuade me to open it.

CONTENTS

INTRODUCTION

Once upon a time, the story goes, two writers walked into a producer's office in Hollywood and sold a script by saying just three words: 'Jaws in Space.' That script was to become the blockbuster movie *Alien*, and that moment has passed into Hollywood mythology as the perfect pitch.

I call pitching the 'great accelerator'. The ability to pitch well is essential for anyone who wants to speed up their career as a writer, producer or director in cinema or TV anywhere in the world. Indeed, today the pitch is becoming increasingly important for all artists, including novelists, journalists and playwrights.

Pitching will not only help sell your ideas but develop them in the first place. It helps you clarify character and refine plot. It makes it easier to collaborate with others. Every good writer, director and producer I know is excellent at pitching.

However, there are also many myths about pitching. One is that to pitch is to put on an act – to distort the work of the true artist. In fact, good pitching means being true to yourself, your own culture and values. I've taught writers, directors and producers from all over the world to pitch successfully while staying true to themselves. In this book, you'll learn how to pitch powerfully as yourself, whoever you are and wherever you come from.

The content is based on my own experience as an award-winning writer-director and from teaching hundreds of writers and filmmakers over the years. It combines solid content with personal stories from my own career and from fellow industry professionals.

Whatever your goal in film or television (or elsewhere in the arts) *Jaws in Space* will take you through the process of creating a professional pitch from beginning to end. You'll find a series of practical techniques and exercises, from how to develop a compelling log line to advanced skills that will help you in all kinds of pitching situations. You'll learn the special requirements for pitching multi-stranded films, TV series and documentaries. Then we'll follow through the process of taking a pitch meeting and discuss powerful ways of ensuring you perform at your best whether presenting to a single person or a large audience.

It will also give guidance as to how you can continue to develop your skills as your confidence grows.

This book grew out of the segments on developing your premise and marketing your script in my earlier book *Teach Yourself: Complete Screenwriting Course*. *Jaws in Space*, however, also contains material that is not in the first book, with room to dig deeper into important areas that had to be left out before. And when you've worked through *Jaws in Space*, you'll find that *Teach Yourself: Complete Screenwriting Course* will take you forward, through the process of writing the treatments you'll need, developing character and structure, writing a new screenplay or series proposal and editing it to a high standard. Indeed, if you seriously want to become adept at creating scripts, whether as a writer or as someone who works with writers, I suggest the two books will work very well together.

THE ART OF THE PITCH

Where does pitching come from? People have been pitching to each other for thousands of years – well before the first Stone Age artists talked their friends into helping out with the latest cave painting. Humans have long used spoken language to convince, persuade and avoid nasty consequences.

Literary agent Julian Friedmann believes film pitching as it now exists developed around the mid twentieth century. At that time, the Writers Guild of America was so powerful in Hollywood that no screenwriter would write a proposal for a studio without being paid. So, to save money, a producer might wander down to where the writers were working and ask them to 'tell' him a story on the spot. Over time, both writers and producers became skilled at telling and listening to shortened versions of future scripts.

However pitching came about, beware of another myth. This is the scene in the movies where a writer pitches his new script to a studio exec. He describes the opening, in glowing terms. Draws the executive into his world. Widens his hands as he moves into the main story, holds the man spellbound for ten or fifteen minutes as the strands interweave...

This is not the reality.

The good – and bad – news is that nobody has ten or fifteen minutes to weave their pitch. The most important part of your pitch is the first sentence – the first two at the most. It's what's known in the business world as the 'elevator pitch' – for when you meet your target in a lift and have to pitch in the time available before he steps out at the next floor. In the industry, it's also known as your **log line** or **premise**.

This is good news in that you don't have to perform at length, but bad news in that you have to be able to express the essence of your script in just a very few words. If this makes your heart sink, let me reassure you. You are not alone. We've all been there, many times. However, as we'll see, creating that one- or two-sentence pitch need not be as complicated as you think. There are very practical and effective techniques you can use to find the very heart of your story.

Having said that, it does take commitment and a desire to settle for only the very best you can produce.

Why just one or two sentences? Isn't that an unfair restriction on us creative artists? Would Shakespeare have been expected to describe *Hamlet* in the Elizabethan equivalent of a lift? Well, possibly, yes. He, too, worked in a competitive and somewhat cut-throat business where those with power had little time for waffle.

The one-sentence pitch exists for a very good reason. Despite the fortunes spent on advertising, PR, star actors, awards and social media, the truth is that there is only one thing that reliably gets people to queue up at the cinema or download the latest must-watch series, and that's word of mouth. Most viewing decisions are based on a recommendation by a trusted friend.

And when a friend tells you about a good film or TV programme, they don't have ten to fifteen minutes to describe every detail from opening fade up to closing fade to black. They have a sentence or two, while you message each other, chat at the coffee machine or wait for a bus.

Furthermore, today's market is tougher than it has ever been. Audiences have more and more demands on their time and many alternative ways of entertaining themselves, from YouTube videos, streaming music and the whole spectrum of social media, to online and offline games, books (printed and electronic), live theatre plays, concerts, sports events or simply chilling out at the local bar or restaurant.

Your film, single drama or series has to be so compelling that it can compete with all those and more.

When you pitch to a producer, financier or agent, they are – consciously or unconsciously – imagining these competitors, those conversations. They're asking themselves whether your idea is strong enough for one friend to convince another that it's worth buying a ticket or spending money on the box set – or whatever it takes for your project to be a success.

That is the starting point of everything. Call it a pitch, log line or premise, it all grows from that word of mouth.

How do you get to do that? Well, that's what most of the rest of this book is about. But first, a word of warning. There is a certain magic in creativity. There are matters that can't be forced into existence. Artists give this magic different names – the Muse, inspiration, luck, genius... Part of becoming adept at any art, whether writing or directing, or indeed producing, is learning when to stand back and watch the magic happen.

When I started in the industry, I pitched non-stop and sold nothing. Clearly, the film industry wasn't ready to appreciate my genius.

Then, one day, I pitched an idea to a producer and something different occurred. I saw it first in his eyes. I'd struck a nerve. I had stumbled on what screenwriting guru Linda Aronson calls *the spark*. The spark is the very essence of a good pitch – it's that special something that catches fire in the listener. It can't be legislated for or created by rote. It's part of the magic. And you find it, more often than not, through sheer good luck. Once I'd seen the spark in that producer's eyes, I never wanted to pitch an idea without it again.

You can't demand that the spark appears, but you can entice it in. You do it through sheer hard work and application, using every skill you can draw on, polishing the diamond of your pitch and trying it on people until – sometimes when you least expect it – someone's eyes light up. The processes in this book will help you find the magic. No techniques can force inspiration to come, but they can lay down the groundwork. As Kevin Costner's character says in *Field of Dreams* – 'If you build it, he will come.' Or as golfer Gary Player put it, 'I've been very lucky in my life – and the harder I worked, the luckier I got.'

Some would-be artists worry about techniques and exercises. They become anxious that they will somehow stifle their creativity. However, the reverse is the case. I suggest you think of the techniques as recipes. Recipes aren't straitjackets; they are processes through which you can express your very special, individual work. The same recipe for, say, lasagne or chocolate cake can be used to make something very ordinary or something exquisite. The difference is the flair and personality you bring to it and the quality and freshness of the ingredients you choose.

As you go through your career, you'll find yourself pitching to all kinds of people – from producers, development executives and financiers to interns and office juniors, not to mention actors, directors, friends, fellow writers and of course agents. You'll pitch to them all in more or less the same way. Agents won't buy your script, but want to know it can be pitched to someone who will. So they will be listening for the same things that any production executive would. The major difference is that an agent is not just interested in whether you have one good idea, but whether you will continue to have good ideas and write good scripts for years to come. They are taking the long view.

For ease of reading, therefore, I'm mostly going to refer to the person being pitched to as a producer or exec, although in most cases what you read will apply equally to agents, script editors, distributors, financiers, co-writers, actors, crew members – in fact just about anyone you can get to listen to your pitch.

Similarly, as the person pitching, you may be a writer or director. Or you may be a producer, pitching to a co-producer, distributor or financier. Or you may be an agent yourself. For most purposes, the issues and techniques are very similar, so most of the time I'm going to refer to the pitcher as a writer.

Finally, this is an equal opportunities book. Sometimes I'll refer to the person being pitched to as *she* and sometimes as *he*. And occasionally as *they*. For variety.

TO SUM UP...

- The most important part of your pitch is the first sentence.
- Most audience decisions come down to word of mouth.
- To pitch is to imagine a conversation between possible viewers.
- Work hard and the magic will come.

THE PITCH RELATIONSHIP: **YOU**

There are two sides to any pitch – you and them – the pitcher and the pitched to. Both have needs and will need to have them fulfilled if the relationship is going to be a productive and happy one.

In this chapter, we're going to look at you – the pitcher. What is your role in the proceedings?

The first step is to realise that pitching is not about asking for favours. Without you – or someone like you – producers have nothing to produce. You aren't coming to them to beg for help – you are offering them a chance to collaborate with you on a venture that could be good for both of you. Of course, you need them, but as we'll see in the next chapter, they need you too.

This doesn't mean you should put on airs. It means you may need to change your mindset. You may be an artist but you have invested your own time and money in this script. You've paid the bills, fed and clothed yourself. You're as much a business person as the producer you're pitching to.

However, many beginners go into a pitch with only the vaguest idea of what kind of business relationship they want to get into. They know having a producer is an important part of getting their film or programme made, but haven't thought through what they really want.

But if you don't know what you want, how do you know whether the person you are pitching to is able to give it to you? How do you even know if they are the right person – and how do you know what questions to ask?

In the next chapter, we're going to talk about what the producer wants to hear. Here, we talk about the importance of knowing what you want.

YOUR NEEDS AND VALUES

....

EXERCISE

Take a moment to write down what you want from this project. Goals such as *getting it made, a screen credit, fame, exposing corruption, experience, making a difference, making people laugh, making money...* Don't use my words, choose your own – and keep each item short, a bullet point of one, two or three words. Spend some time on this – you'll discover some important insights into what really drives your work.

When you've done that, look over your list and number your values in order of priority from one (the highest priority) downwards.

There is no right or wrong answer to this question – your priorities are your own concern. Only you can decide what your values are – but you'll need to know what they are.

....

This exercise is important because different producers will be right for different goals. You may, for example, find that one producer has the track record to get your script onto the screen, but won't pay you upfront. Another might pay well, but has a weaker track record. A third, on the other hand, may pay well, have the power to get the film made, but suggest changes that distort your original ideas out of shape.

Initially, you'll probably want to pitch to anyone and everyone and be delighted if anyone even listens, let alone takes you seriously. However, even at this stage you should go into meetings with your eyes open. Research the producer, company or agent. Check their credits and what they've said on the record, and find out what they like to make and how they like to make it. Knowing your highest priorities will help guide you. (There's more on researching your targets in 'The Pitch Relationship: Them'.)

And when you get to pitch to them, your priorities will also help you know what to ask for, where to stick and where to be flexible.

Of course, your priorities will change over time. A first-time writer will probably accept a less than perfect deal in order to get a foothold in the business. Later, with a track record under your belt, you might want to hold out for terms that are closer to your vision.

WHEN TO PITCH?

Time for another reality check. Unless you have a track record, you will not sell a fiction idea purely on the basis of one meeting. However great your pitch, a producer will always want to read the script.

You might be great at pitching and lousy at writing. You might be great at writing, but this particular idea simply doesn't work when you try to write it. There may be hidden plot holes, waiting like landmines to explode once you expand the idea to its full length. Many a great pitch has given birth to a dire damp squib of a screenplay.

Dan O'Bannon and Ronald Shusett had already written 85 per cent of the script for *Alien* when they delivered their three-word pitch, 'Jaws in Space'. Furthermore, O'Bannon had already made a successful low-budget sci-fi movie with John Carpenter, *Dark Star*.

So, in fact, your goal in pitching is not to sell the script on the spot. Your goal is for the producer to say one of two simple phrases:

Tell me more.

Or, better still:

Send me the script.

This leads to one of the most important rules of pitching:

Never pitch a fiction script to a buyer before it's finished.

Because, if you hook a producer or agent with a great pitch, he'll want to read it now. Not in a month's time. Certainly not in six months or a year. If he has to wait, he'll start to cool down. By the time you deliver the script, he may well have moved on to a new project, allocated those funds to a different film or possibly even changed jobs. Even if he is still in the market for scripts such as yours, the story you pitched to him all those months ago will now sound so last year!

I once worked with a producer who'd developed a great pitch for a movie. She flew to Cannes, raised strong interest and came to a provisional agreement with two financiers. But she didn't have a script to show them. So she returned home and commissioned a writer, who wrote two drafts. The second draft still needed work, so she brought me on for two further drafts. By now, a year had passed. When she went back to her financiers with a polished screenplay, one had given up waiting and put all his money into a different film. The other had left the film business altogether. She'd lost two golden opportunities, all because she pitched without a script.

You only get one chance with each person you pitch to. Which means you have to make it your best shot. So the script shouldn't only be finished; it should be as good as possible. That means you absolutely must get at least one professional script report from a reader or company you trust, and allow time to put their recommendations into action.

Personally, I commission at least two full reports on all my screenplays – using different readers. Because telling stories on screen is a collaborative art and nobody, however good, can see all the possible angles or elephant traps in any given script.

So, if you hear the golden words *send me the script* you should be in a position to comply fast. At best, you can probably squeeze out a delay of a week or two by saying you are just putting in some final touches. But it had better not be longer than that.

WHEN TO PITCH (2)?

Actually, I'm going to qualify that immediately. There are times when you absolutely must pitch scripts you haven't yet written! You will learn enormously from crafting a pitch at the very start and getting a response (or lack of it). It will save you enormous trouble and avoid wasting time on work that will never get produced.

But how do you do this, without blowing your chances of a future sale?

The trick, at this early stage, is to avoid pitching to anyone you actually want to sell the screenplay to. Particularly useful people to try out your early pitches on would be:

- Producers who work in different genres.

- Distributors – they sell finished movies and TV programmes to the cinemas and TV channels in different parts of the world.

- Sales agents – not to be confused with writers' agents, sales agents represent producers and sell the finished films and programmes to the distributors. They generally cover the whole world and often get involved with helping raise finance in advance of production.

(We'll look at how you get to them later, in 'Making the Approach'.)

When I went to Cannes with my co-producers on what would become my debut movie, *Paradise Grove*, we pitched to everyone we met, including major sales agents and distributors. We learned from everybody. More importantly, one sales agent and one major Hollywood producer became good friends. Each year, when we're back in Cannes, I make a point of meeting up and having a drink. Neither relationship has resulted directly in work – yet – but the advice and contacts that have come from them have been invaluable.

What if you want to pitch for development money to pay you to write the script in the first place? The harsh fact is that development money is hard to find, particularly if you don't have a track record. Developing a script is high risk, and brings poor returns. Most screenplays that go into development never get made and therefore never recoup their investment. It's almost impossible to tell which ideas will lead to a filmable script and which will sink without trace. Furthermore, in the process, conflicts can arise between producers and writers over how the script should progress.

For this reason, even experienced writers will often choose to develop their scripts themselves, 'on spec'. They prefer the freedom to write the story in the way they want, to allow it to change and evolve without the pressure of a producer waiting for results. And you will generally be paid more for a script that is already written.

After all this, if you do want development funding, there are a very few development funds around – mostly backed by regional or national agencies – such as the BFI, Creative England, The EU's Media Fund, Medienboard in Berlin and Screen Australia. These are almost invariably set up to support a particular geographical area, so you'll need to research the agencies that cater for the area where you live or work.

But I'll repeat, development money is hard to get. Don't wait for it. Get writing. Keep the day job. Beg, borrow and steal what it takes to pay your bills. And pitch the finished script.

WHEN TO PITCH (3)?

Things are different when it comes to documentary. A documentary script will probably be written in post-production after filming is complete, so you have no choice but to pitch without one. However, you should still plan the project as much as possible and be ready to send a detailed proposal (see 'Visuals and Leave-behinds'). In addition, developing your project in detail will protect you. There is no copyright in ideas but there is copyright protection in the way you develop those ideas and the words with which you write them down.

WHEN TO PITCH (4)?

There is one final time you may find yourself pitching an idea without a finished script. As we'll see later, you may find a producer passes on your first pitch and asks, 'What else have you got?'

Ideally, you should have some alternative scripts ready to pitch instead. However, if you have a good idea that you haven't yet developed and the rapport in the room has been good, you may well decide to take the risk.

But I'm moving too deeply into the pitch meeting, which I'll explore in more detail in 'The Pitch Meeting'.

Because it's time to look at that person at the other end of the pitch – the pitchee.

TO SUM UP...

- Know what your priorities are.
- Only pitch fiction stories to buyers when you have a polished script ready to send.
- Before then, test your pitch on people who aren't your main targets.
- For documentaries, have a detailed proposal ready to send.
- Sometimes you may be asked what else you've got.

THE PITCH RELATIONSHIP: **THEM**

Then there's the person on the other end of the pitch. The one whom you want to impress. Who will you be pitching to, where do you find them and what do they want to hear?

WHO TO PITCH TO

Your main targets will depend on who you are and what stage you've reached in your career. However, everyone has one thing in common: we all want to pitch to the person who makes the decisions.

As a writer pitching for cinema, you'll mostly be pitching to producers. They may be independent producers, working alone or with a partner, or staff producers in larger production companies or one of the studios, which have offices in the US and overseas.

Independent or staff producers will also be important targets for TV scripts, as well as commissioning editors in charge of specific programme strands at the major channels.

However, if you don't have much of a track record – or, indeed, any track record at all – you may well be talking to people a long way from the decision maker. This could be a development executive, script editor, script reader or even an intern. Or you might find yourself pitching to someone with an impressive title (such as Head of Development), but that doesn't necessarily mean they can make buying decisions. She may have to pitch in turn to a senior executive, possibly the CEO.

However, anyone and everyone should be pitched to seriously. Don't make the mistake of thinking you are too important for the 17-year-old unpaid assistant who wasn't born when all your favourite movies were made. That intern may well have more clout than you think. Every project needs a supporter inside the production company, studio or channel, and you never know who will become that driving force.

Be aware, too, that today's intern may become tomorrow's leading producer, Head of Drama at the BBC or studio boss, and if you build a strong relationship now it may stand you in good stead in the future.

Pitching is not just for Christmas. Pitching is about establishing relationships that can last for decades.

DO YOU NEED AN AGENT?

Being taken on by an agent is useful, but not essential. Many successful screenwriters manage without an agent altogether. A good agent will help guide you, suggest ways to develop your career, give feedback on your writing, know the best people to send your scripts to and negotiate the deals when you make a sale. And some production companies will only consider submissions if they come from a recognised agent or a writer with a substantial track record.

However, an agent isn't your mother. She will have to divide her time between all her clients, so don't expect a continual flow of guidance and suggestions, or feedback on every draft. Her suggestions for your career may be useful. But she only knows what's selling at the time.

One writer I know says that if your agent tells you to write sci-fi, make sure the next script you write is anything but. By the time you've finished it, everyone will be so swamped with sci-fi scripts that they'll be desperate to read something different.

Overstated, perhaps, but there is more than a grain of truth in what he says.

Nor is an agent a sure-fire route to the top. You will still need to go out, find producers and pitch. Julian Friedmann, my current agent, has arranged meetings for me here and in Hollywood, sold my scripts, brought me commissions and given me his heartfelt advice. Some of that advice I've taken and some I haven't. Some of my scripts he's loved and some he's hated. But I've also had to go out and find producers for myself.

As I mentioned earlier, pitching to an agent is substantially the same as pitching to a producer. The primary difference is that he's interested in more than a single project. He's thinking in terms of your career. As well as a sparkling, well-polished script you'll need to show that you have other ideas for further scripts, possibly in different genres and for different markets. He knows that a writer rarely survives on one kind of screenplay but needs to have a mind that can apply itself to a wide range of productions, from TV soaps upwards.

WHERE DO YOU FIND PEOPLE TO PITCH TO?

Finding the right people to pitch to takes time, effort and perseverance – and most of all research.

Look for producers and agents who feel right for your project. Maybe they work in the same genre, or budget area, or have shown an interest in a relevant genre in an interview. Make a point of watching as many appropriate films and programmes as you can. Make a note of the producer credits and the production company and check out their websites.

It's vital that you find a specific name to approach – generalised approaches to a production company, an agency, or even those to a job title, such as 'Head of Development', will be at best sent to the bottom of the pile and at worst ignored.

Online databases such as IMDb, Cinando, Broadcast and Screen Daily (run by the trade magazine *Screen International*) provide invaluable information on individual producers and agents. *Screen*

International also runs regular articles both online and in print which are invaluable for researching names of cinema producers and *Broadcast* does the same for TV. While almost all these sites offer basic services and information for free, a subscription will unlock a wealth of further information and regular email and print updates.

There are also excellent print and online film industry directories – in particular Kays, The Knowledge, KFTV and Mandy – which you can find on the net and in the reference sections of good local libraries and the BFI library in London. These all have sections which list many, though not all, production companies and agents. The fullest list of agents in the UK can be found in the current *Writers' and Artists' Yearbook*. (I've included details of all these in the resources section at the end of this book.)

When you find the names of individual producers and development executives, check further to see what else they've worked on. Most companies, and many producers and agents, now have their own Twitter feeds and Facebook pages. A web search will often bring up interviews with newspapers, industry magazines and blogs. Study these for any comments that will show their attitude, the kind of material they're looking for, the programmes they like or even how they like to be approached.

Agents will normally list their personal clients on their website, which can help you find which agent will be right for you to approach. You can also search the names of specific writers in your genre to see who represents them.

....

EXERCISE – **START A HIT LIST**

Keep a well-organised list of what you find and life will be much easier later, when it comes to pitch.

Different writers work differently. Some like to have a spreadsheet on their computer or phone – others prefer a physical card index, or an A–Z phone book. Whatever your preference, you will need something in which you can keep updated notes on whom to contact, how to contact them, why they are appropriate for you and your project, and later on what their response has been.

I personally use a very simple Open Office spreadsheet, with one producer or company per line, so that I can get a very quick overview of where I am at any one point. I have a column for contact details, and one for the date of the last approach, whether I've had a response, etc. Another column gives a brief note of their relevant productions and any other useful background notes. I can highlight those I want to contact next – choosing appropriate colours for my highest priorities.

In this way, I don't have to waste time reminding myself where I'm up to each time I open the file. Believe me, after a few searches, emails or phone calls, you'll soon struggle to remember what you found and who said what. You must write it down in a form you can easily access when you need it. You'll also want to continue researching possible new targets over the next months and years, adding their names to the list as you go.

....

TO SUM UP...

- You'll be pitching to a wide range of people from independent producers to development executives in large companies and studios.
- Pitching is about establishing long-term relationships.
- Take every pitch seriously; you never know which lowly intern may rise to become a valuable high-level contact in the future.
- Having an agent can be useful but it's not essential.
- There are many resources online and in print to help you create your hit list – start building one now.

WHAT THEY WANT

Earlier we looked at why you wanted to pitch. Now we need to look at the other side of the story. What of the pitchee? What does she want out of the relationship?

The easy answer is that she wants to make a film or TV programme (or, in the case of an agent, find someone who does). But on its own that's not going to get us very far. How do you convince her that she should choose your script, rather than anyone else's?

Of course, you know yours is brilliantly written. (You've had at least two professional reports, haven't you? And acted upon them.) So what does she need to hear that's going to make her say *'Send me the script'* – so that she can see how brilliant it is for herself.

Producers are constantly being asked what they are looking for, in interviews and at industry panel events. The trouble is, the answer is almost always the same and almost always vague. She'll say (a) she doesn't have any fixed rules, (b) she'll know when she sees it and (c) she wants something that excites her.

So much is true: the film and TV industry runs on celluloid and pixels, paper (loads of paper) and excitement. A script is produced because people get so excited that they buy it, financiers get so excited that they finance it, star actors get so excited that they agree to work for less than their normal rates, and director, cast and crew get so excited that they work long hours in difficult conditions. What you are pitching isn't three-act structure, or clever characters, or even exquisite dialogue – it's excitement.

But what they don't tell you is that, before they get excited about your pitch, every single producer must answer yes to five very specific questions. These questions are so crucial that failing any of them will mean that your script has almost no chance of being read at all.

So let's look at each question in turn. In real life, these questions don't come in a given order – they are all equally important. But the first one on our list focuses on the producer's own specific situation in life.

QUESTION A: IS IT APPROPRIATE?

Does your pitch fit her career plans? Is it the kind of film she wants to make, or be seen to make? Or is it the kind of programme she's been employed to find? Is it right for what her company produces or is planning to produce in the future?

One producer may be looking for projects that are within her reach – probably low-budget, for local consumption, using the contacts she has in her city. Another may want more expensive, mainstream co-productions, to enable her to maintain a cash flow and pay for her office and staff. Yet another may be on the lookout for programmes that will win her awards and the kudos that comes with them.

There's not much joy to be had from pitching a low-budget horror flick to a studio looking for high-end romantic comedies. Nor in trying to sell an international nature documentary series idea to an independent who has built a niche making micro-budget teen dramas.

It looks amateurish to approach a producer with a script or documentary idea that they would never consider in a million years. So you need to do your homework. As we saw in the last chapter, there is no excuse for not checking a producer's website, googling their credits and looking for interviews or blogs.

Having said that, a word of warning. Just because a producer has concentrated on edgy, low-budget horror movies for ten years doesn't mean they're not considering a change. They may indeed now be looking for that mainstream rom-com that will give them an entry into the North American market. However, even here, research may tease that out. An interview for *Screen International* or the *Guardian* may drop a few hints as to how they're planning for the future.

For this reason, you'll see when we talk about the pitch meeting that I recommend starting with a few targeted questions. Ask what kinds of projects they've been developing. What films and programmes they've liked recently. You may be surprised at what they say.

If the worst comes to the worst and you find you were about to pitch a project that is clearly not going to work for them, you still have time to shift direction and pitch another project (you will have some other ideas up your sleeve, won't you?).

QUESTION B: IS IT RIGHT FOR THE BUDGET?

Here's another of those myths. Read almost any book on film or TV production and it will tell you how a producer estimates a production budget. First, she calculates how much to spend on the major creative elements – star actors, director, herself as producer, and of course the script. These are called the 'above the line' costs. Then she counts the number of locations, decides how long is needed for filming, how many crew members, how much equipment, set building, transport, catering, editing, sound design, publicity and so forth, down to the smallest nail, and puts these costs 'below the line'. Finally, she adds the above- and below-the-line figures together and that's what she makes the film for.

It sounds convincing but in fact it's a fantasy. The reality is that a producer looks at the project and tries to guess how much she'll be able to sell it for. That's her budget.

The key question now becomes: does your script fit the budget?

No producer will stay in business very long if she makes films that cost more than she sells them for. Now, of course, this is mainly guesswork. Nobody can accurately predict whether a film will make a profit or a loss. Indeed, most films don't make their money back. Some years ago, Barclays Bank analysed the finances of a wide range of cinema films across all genres and budgets. They revealed that, on average, out of any ten movies produced, five will make a loss, three will break even, one will make a small profit and the lucky tenth will earn enough to pay for all the rest. So filmmaking most closely resembles a session of Russian roulette, only with worse odds: five chances in ten of going broke.

THE FOUR QUADRANTS

However, there are a few basic principles. The first is known as the Four Quadrants. According to this, the movie market for adults (as opposed to children) divides into four.

In the first quadrant we find males between the ages of 14 and 24. They are relatively easy to please with fast-moving stories, violence, gross-out humour and wet T-shirts. They go to the cinema most often, watch the most trailers and buy the two most profitable commodities on the planet – popcorn and Coca-Cola. This last point is more relevant than you might think, as most movies don't make a profit from selling cinema tickets. The theatrical (cinema) screening is primarily a shop window, to build sales in other media – DVD, Blu-ray, streaming and downloads and ultimately TV. And in-house catering.

It may sound very hard-nosed to say your artistically dazzling script is being judged according to whether enough people will buy snacks when it's showing. However, that's how the industry works.

And along with that thought comes the question of the length of your script. Mainstream cinemas hate movies that last much more than two hours. However brilliantly made, a two-and-a-half or three-hour movie means fewer performances per day. This inevitably reduces the number of tickets they can sell. Next time a highly praised – but long – movie appears in the cinema, watch out for how long it stays. Most, even the most prestigious, disappear within two or three weeks, leaving shorter (and possibly poorer) movies to mop up the audiences the longer films couldn't stay around to reach.

The second quadrant comprises females between 14 and 24. They are more discriminating. However, they also like to go to the movies more frequently than older audiences and will often accompany their boyfriends.

The third quadrant brings us men aged 25 and over. That's it. There is currently no upper category for cinemagoers. Once you are 25, the movie industry considers you old.

Men in this quadrant are more likely to be in a long-term relationship, may well have children, almost certainly go to the cinema less often (work, the need for babysitters, etc). Because they don't go so much, they're more discriminating. They probably rely on reviews to guide them and they are, of course, less likely to see the trailers.

Finally, and most difficult to reach of all, is the fourth quadrant – women of 25 and over. Because they don't even believe the reviews.

It probably won't have escaped your notice that the first two quadrants more or less correspond to the majority of the multiplex audience and the third and fourth to the independent market – sometimes called specialist, niche or art-house. Of course, this is a broad generalisation but the essential point remains: while older audiences do go to see multiplex movies and younger audiences to the independent screens, by and large the multiplex audience is under 24 and the specialist cinema audience will be older.

What does this mean to the producer listening to your pitch? Well, she's listening for anything in your script that will be expensive. The more locations in your story, the more the film will cost, especially if they involve much travel. Special effects aren't cheap, even in these days of computer-generated graphics (CGI). Certain situations are especially demanding – such as night filming, filming at sea, a period setting. And large casts or big set-piece scenes. An expensive movie must play to the largest audiences to make its money back.

This doesn't mean that it has to be crass or appeal to the lowest common denominator. Quite the opposite: brash and nasty movies will often go straight to video, while some of the highest-rated movies ever made were aimed specifically at the mass market – movies such as *Rear Window*, *The Searchers*, *Lawrence of Arabia*, *Goodfellas*, *An Officer and a Gentleman*, *When Harry Met Sally* and

The Sixth Sense. Although it's fair to note that many of these were made before the rise of the blockbuster.

What it does mean is that, if your script is likely to be expensive to produce, it will need the elements that appeal to the multiplex audience – and primarily that means ages 14–24: wide emotional appeal, a strong storyline, exciting roles that will draw top stars to act in it and eye-catching visuals.

However, don't fall into the trap of thinking that the art-house market is a safety net for movies that didn't make it in the multiplexes. Art-house audiences have their own demands. They are less interested in star actors, but follow star directors, such as David Lynch, Abbas Kiarostami or Pedro Almodóvar. They expect stories which are edgier, perhaps darker, or with a distinctive style. Films with challenging thematic content do well in this market, as do films which play more overtly with the form.

But the smaller art-house audiences mean your script must be capable of being made on a much smaller budget: fewer locations, smaller cast and crew, maybe a cameo role for a star name to help publicity, few if any special effects. Most of all, a story that's strong enough to hold its own without the extra production value that money can bring.

You may well have heard of so-called 'Four-Quadrant' movies – that is, films which manage to appeal across the board. They do exist: films such as *Titanic* or *Meet the Parents*. There are also 'break-out' films, which begin as low-budget movies and break out of their niche to a much larger audience: films such as *Amélie*, *The Full Monty* and *The Blair Witch Project*. However, none of these movies was expected to break so big. Indeed, while you'll certainly read of producers who say they are planning a Four-Quadrant film, the truth is that you can't. If audiences were so predictable, we'd all be millionaires. The most obvious success-bait can plummet to obscurity while a niche story can suddenly catch fire. William Goldman, screenwriter of *Butch Cassidy and the Sundance Kid*, puts it best when it comes to box-office success: 'Nobody knows anything… Not one person in the entire motion picture field knows for a certainty what's going to work. Every time out it's a guess and, if you're lucky, an educated one.'

One great danger in trying to appeal to everyone is that you fall between the two stools of multiplex and art-house and produce what a Miramax executive once described to me as a 'tweener movie'. This has nothing to do with age but describes the no-man's land 'between' one audience and the other. Also called an 'on-the-bridge' film.

One of the most famous examples of an on-the-bridge movie was *My Big Fat Greek Wedding*. This was, and is, an entertaining romantic comedy about an American-Greek woman who falls in love with a non-Greek man. However, despite being produced by Tom Hanks, for a long time no distributor would touch it. The problem was audience – it was neither big enough for the multiplexes nor stylish or oddball enough for the art-house circuit. In the end, the movie took a very long time to build its audience, step by step, with the writer (also lead actress) reportedly hosting coffee mornings for local Greek communities every time it opened in a new state.

Many tweener or on-the-bridge films are not so lucky and end up on-the-shelf.

Just about everything I've said about movies applies equally to TV. Independent producers have to sell their programmes or programme ideas to the broadcasters. And while in-house producers and commissioning editors may not actually have to 'sell' their productions in the same way as an external producer, they still have to follow budget guidelines and attract the appropriate number of viewers for the money they spend.

Here, too, you find mainstream – primetime on the largest network channels – and independent – obscure time slots, smaller channels, cable and satellite. Even for the mainstream, primetime slots, budgets tend to be lower. For the more expensive dramas, such as *War and Peace* or the nature documentary series *Planet Earth*, producers will almost invariably need to find co-finance from other broadcasters and will therefore be looking for broad-based audience appeal.

Some channels become known for trying out adventurous, low-budget, niche productions – such as Channel 4 with series such as

Fresh Meat, E4 with *Skins*, and in the States HBO, developing series such as *The Shield* and *Breaking Bad*.

It's not yet clear where subscription channels such as Sky and video on demand (VOD) platforms such as Netflix and Amazon Prime fit into the mix, but at present they are mainly backing relatively expensive, high-profile series, such as *House of Cards*, with the aim of attracting a broad range of new subscribers.

What this all boils down to is not that you need to know your precise budget – or indeed your detailed audience demographic. Nor should you try desperately to pitch a script to fit the market. You should certainly never say anything like 'This will appeal to a wide audience' or 'It will make a fortune'.

You should develop the best script you possibly can – and pitch it with a professional understanding of where it will play.

QUESTION C: IS IT CINEMATIC (OR TELEVISUAL)?

In other words, does your story work for the screen? However good your ideas, however appropriate for a particular company, however right for their future market, this is a deal breaker.

There is a vast and often misunderstood difference between novels, plays and short stories, on the one hand, and stories told on screen – whether fictional or documentary, for cinema, TV or other media such as the internet – on the other. While at first glance they may seem related, they work in entirely different ways. As different as, say, a painting is from an opera.

The usual way of describing the difference is that film is 'visual'. However, the term visual can be misleading. Certainly, your pitch must create pictures in the listener's mind, but this doesn't mean that your story has to be filled with physical action, fights, chases and shoot-outs. It means we're looking for a story that can play out in front of our eyes. This normally demands a strongly motivated protagonist, whose struggle to attain his goal moves forward in a way that can be *visualised*.

Steve Jobs tells the story of the man who developed Apple computers. *Spotlight* – the story of a journalistic investigation into covering up child abuse – won the Oscars for best film and best original screenplay in 2016. Also shortlisted that year were *Brooklyn*, the story of a young Irish woman learning to live in 1950s New York, and *Room*, about a mother and son trapped in a single room. Each, in its own way, visualised.

What will ring alarms in the producer's mind is a story that sounds as if it would work better in another medium. For example, a wholly internal struggle that might make a good novel but an undramatic film. Or a discussion of ideas that would work better on stage. In a good screen story, all inner conflict and ideas are externalised in dramatic form – as the clash of characters in pursuit of filmable goals.

To tick this box, the producer needs to be convinced that you understand the nature of the dramatic form and what works on screen.

QUESTION D: IS IT DIFFERENT?

I see many scripts that are perfectly well written, show a strong sense of what's marketable and great cinematic values, yet are totally unsellable because they are simply not different.

Tempting as it may seem, you won't appeal to the market by slavishly copying stories that have been filmed before. You need to bring something fresh and original to the table. A new slant, a personal voice, a surprising angle. You may have studied detective stories or horror movies in depth, but if you don't do something original with your story, you'll find it enormously difficult to break through with your pitch.

Now, you may well argue that cinemas and TV schedules are full of shows that are copies of previous ones – stories that rely on stale formulae. And you'd be right. But here's the thing: they already have writers for these – solid if second-rate writers they can rely on to come up with solid, second-rate scripts.

Your job, as a newcomer, is to provide freshness and originality. Your job is to bring something the hacks can't.

QUESTION E: ARE YOU EMPLOYABLE?

The final question is the flipside of the first. The producer-writer relationship is a delicate one that demands trust on both sides. Now she's asking herself, can you be trusted to do your job professionally?

Are you the kind of writer who believes it's OK to leave plot holes, hoping the rest of the team will spot them, who says, 'The director will solve it'? Or are you conscientious, attending to every tiny detail, submitting only your very best work?

Film is a collaborative art, which means every member of the team must take full responsibility for their work. A contradiction in the story or inconsistency of character may pass unnoticed all the way through to post-production. It may not even get noticed until the film is finished and the reviews come out!

More positively, she's asking what special something you're bringing to the script. What makes you absolutely the right person to be writing it? Is there something in your own story that makes it all the more real? That gives it resonance?

Anything you can provide to bolster your claim will help here. Obviously any credits or track record in film or TV will be useful, but also any writing you've done elsewhere – especially any you've been paid for.

Even if you have no credits on your CV, there are areas you can use – or develop. Are you drawing on your own experiences, do you have relevant expertise or contacts? Can you talk about the research you did for the script? If you haven't already, make a checklist of all the research contacts you've used.

You're a writer – use the skills you have. Start social media accounts that are relevant to your story or genre, sending out informative, useful or entertaining messages. Develop a blog on a related subject, so that you can build your credibility and gain a following.

Anything here will not only help reassure the producer that you can write with authenticity and credibility, but also that you could add useful publicity angles when the film is eventually released. Publicity which, of course, will be useful for your own career prospects, too.

When you pitch to a producer you are pitching yourself. What the producer is buying, as much as anything else, is you. Your passion for your script. Your confidence in it. Your voice.

....

EXERCISE – **YOUR PERSONAL LOG LINE**

In the next chapters, you'll see how you create a compelling log line which will be the heart of your pitch. However, you also need a log line for yourself. You will constantly be introducing yourself to people, whether in person, on paper or in an email, and nothing comes over worse than a stumbling description of yourself that rambles for too long, fails to highlight your strengths or trails to an embarrassed halt. Or all of the above.

Write down what makes you most employable. Start with your job description. It doesn't matter that you may not have sold anything. If you are writing or have written a script, then you are a writer. If you are planning to direct or putting together a project, you have every right to call yourself a director or producer.

Next add any experience. If you already work in the industry, even as a runner, that still shows that you are already on the ladder. If not, then what relevant life experience do you have? What research have you carried out? Say you're developing a medical drama. Have you worked in the field? Or can you at least say you have close research contacts in local hospitals and GP surgeries?

If you feel you have little to put in your log line, then you should plan to create more. What can you build on? Can you use your existing skills to bolster your CV?

Some writers like to write short films, short stories or fringe theatre plays. Is there a local group where you can get your work produced? A magazine that could print your stories? Enter your work for competitions. Consider starting a blog based on the subject of your script.

Here are some example personal log lines to get you going:

I'm a screenwriter with three feature scripts in development.

I'm a writer of short stories and have worked for ten years as a social worker, helping rehabilitate young drug addicts.

I'm a writer-director of three award-nominated short films.

I'm the creator of CrimInt, a blog on real-life crime based on my research.

....

TO SUM UP...

* Producers are looking for ideas that excite them. However, before they go any further they must satisfy five key questions:

    Is it appropriate for them?
    Is the budget right for the project?
    Is it cinematic?
    Is it different?
    Are you employable – why are you the best person to have written this script?

* Start writing your personal log line.

THE PITCH TEMPLATE – INTRODUCTION

To recap, the job of the pitch is to excite producers and answer their five most important questions – and all this in a single sentence, or two at the most.

It sounds impossible and yet writers, directors and producers do it every day of the week. 'Jaws in Space' achieved it in just three words. It offered a movie that was **appropriate** to the producer's needs. It would clearly **not** be **cheap** – yet promised a **wide appeal**. The idea was **cinematic** – creating pictures in the listener's mind from the start – and **different** – we'd seen *Jaws* but not 'Jaws in Space'. Finally, the professionalism and brevity of the pitch went a long way to proving that **the writers knew their job**.

In a moment, we're going to look at a standard template for an **Advanced Pitch Sentence** that will be your default position for almost every pitch you ever need to make. It may seem simple at first glance but it is enormously flexible and can be applied to most films and TV programmes, fiction or documentary.

Earlier, I emphasised you will not be able to sell your script on the pitch alone. That the real goal of a pitch is for the buyer to say 'Send me the script'. Think about this for a moment – it's actually a good thing. It's what makes pitching possible. Because your pitch now becomes very simple.

You no longer have to tell the whole story in your pitch, invoke the complex twists, the subtly interwoven subplots and many complex characters. Producers will read all this in the script itself – which is the best place for them to see it. All the pitch has to do is make them interested enough to want to know more.

It's not how much you can squeeze in – it's how little you can get away with.

Less is more. I've seen many writers snatch defeat from the jaws of victory simply by refusing to shut up and let the producer use his imagination. Remember, too, that at the heart of a good pitch is those two friends standing by the water cooler or at a bus stop talking about a movie one of them saw. Having a conversation.

All good pitching is simply having a conversation.

What we need is a simple, condensed way of getting across the key information in a relaxed, conversational and engaging manner that mirrors how friends talk to each other about the movies and programmes they like.

And luckily, that's exactly what we're going to look at next.

The next three chapters will introduce you to the Advanced Pitch Sentence log line. In the vast majority of cases, this will do everything you want it to. If you're planning or selling a series or multi-stranded story, you'll need to develop two log lines or more – one for the overarching idea of the story or series and at least one or two more for individual episodes or story strands. If you want to see how that works now, jump to chapter 'Series and Multi-stranded Films' and then come back here later.

One of the joys of the Advanced Pitch Sentence is that it's natural and easy to use once you've created it. You don't have to learn anything off by heart, or recite a complicated or clever formula. It can be part of a conversation – which is the point, after all. It provides the listener with all he needs to hear at this stage – in the order he wants to hear it.

....

EXERCISE

To warm up, study as many log lines as you can, especially those in your favourite genres. Writers often ask me where to find log lines to read. The answer is: they're everywhere. Anywhere someone talks or writes about movies or TV programmes. Every review or article will briefly summarise what the story is about – that's basically a log line.

Be careful to distinguish between log lines and **strap lines** (also known as **tag lines**). A strap line is a phrase or sentence used in advertising material, such as a poster. It will generally be more atmospheric than informative. A log line needs to give the essential dramatic pulse of the story. A strap line doesn't. For example, the log line for *Alien* was, as we've seen, 'Jaws in Space'. By contrast, the strap line on the posters was 'In space no one can hear you scream!' Very evocative, but no attempt to say what the story is actually about.

You'll find both strap lines and log lines in advertising copy, on DVD boxes, in Netflix blurbs, on IMDb and any fan blog. Notice which is which and why. You'll also start to pick up log lines in film discussion programmes and on websites. You'll find them in the TV listings and film listings in newspapers and magazines.

Remove or cross out references to star actors and directors. Then judge what's left. Use the same ABCDE questions we looked at in the last chapter. Does this feel *Appropriate* to you as a potential viewer? Does the idea feel like it would be right for its *Budget*? Does it feel like it would work as *Cinema* or *TV*? Does it feel *Different* (or would it have done when it was made)? And, finally, *Employable*: what quality would you expect? Do you trust that it delivers what it says?

Now ask the same questions as if you were a producer, thinking of buying the original script.

....

TO SUM UP...

- All a pitch has to do is entice the listener to read the script.
- It's not how much you can squeeze in, but how little you can get away with.
- The Advanced Pitch Sentence or log line is the easiest way to do this.

GENRE

At some point, whether in a meeting, or over the phone, or even in an email, someone, somewhere is going to ask you to tell them about your story. And you'll start very simply:

'It's a...'

'It's a...' is a relaxed, conversational opening which leads you directly into the first and most urgent thing that the listener needs to know – the genre.

Why genre? The word *genre* comes from French and means 'kind' or 'sort'. So when you tell someone the genre of your project, all you are saying is what kind of project it is – fiction, non-fiction, horror, comedy, thriller, animation, and so on.

Genre is often misunderstood as something that limits a script – as in 'it's only a genre movie'. This is a meaningless phrase. 'Only a genre movie' implies that it's possible for a film to somehow be outside all genres, which leads many writers down an arid, one-way street. Every movie and TV programme – including the greatest works of art – is in one or more genres. Indeed, the best writers and directors are expert at using their genres in fresh and sophisticated ways.

And even if it were possible not to be in a genre, you wouldn't want to be. Genre is all about raising expectations – and expectation is what screen stories are all about. Genre is fundamental to how people decide what to watch and when to watch it. They ask themselves what kind of thing they want to see. Do they feel like a comedy this evening? Or that horror series they've been meaning to watch? Or maybe something more thought-provoking?

So, the first thing that follows *'It's a'* should be the genre – or genres – that you're working in. 'It's a comedy-road movie...' 'It's a science fiction action-adventure...' You have already achieved a number of things in the first five or six words:

- You've established what kind of story you're pitching.

- You've allowed the producer to judge if it's the kind of film he likes to make.

- You've started to engage his imagination by raising expectations.

HOW TO KNOW YOUR GENRE(S)

In many cases this will not be a problem – genre is often obvious, in fact usually more obvious than we expect. You will usually know if you're writing, or aiming to write, a comedy or a horror. However, some stories are less easy to pin down. There are often many different genre elements floating around in any given script.

For example, you're writing a story set in the future that involves a failed footballer who breaks into a bank. It has funny moments, a few shoot-outs, he falls in love with the detective who's on his trail and uses the money he's stolen to help his amateur team win the FA Cup...

Do you pitch it as a crime or gangster story, a sports story, a comedy, an action-adventure, science fiction film or a rom-com – or even (given the shoot-outs) a futuristic Western?

To help us, we're going to need some basic rules of thumb.

RULE OF THUMB 1

First and foremost, genre promises emotion. Comedy promises laughter. Horror promises that you are going to be horrified. A thriller promises to be scary. And so on. Emotion is what we're looking for when we buy a cinema ticket or turn on the TV.

So, your first question should be: what is the most important emotion I want the audience to feel throughout the story. The important word here is 'throughout'. In a good comedy, the audience won't just laugh a bit from time to time or just at the end. They should be laughing all the way through. There will probably be some serious moments, to add contrast, but not many. In a horror story, they will be horrified for most of the running time.

The same applies to all genres – whether thriller (fear), fantasy (wonder) or war film (horror of war). So, the first rule of thumb is to ask which emotions will run throughout your story.

RULE OF THUMB 2

Each genre brings with it the promise of particular motifs. Ideas, characters, situations, even styles that characterise the genre.

A rom-com, for example, will typically centre on a romantically interested couple, something that keeps them apart, inner issues, one of the couple not realising what he or she is rejecting, a scene where they meet in an interesting way, a scene where they argue, a scene where they reconcile and declare their love in front of witnesses, a modern, urban setting, and so forth.

If you create a rom-com that misses out the key elements the audience wants from romantic comedy, you'll find yourself with one very unhappy audience.

So, the second rule is to ask what motifs you have in your story. If you have a gangster at the heart of your TV series, then this could well be a gangster story. If a spaceship, then either sci-fi or space action.

RULE OF THUMB 3

However, there's a catch. If you simply deliver this list of motifs precisely as expected, the audience will find your story predictable. It would seem that you can't win. Damned if you do – damned if you don't.

In fact, you can win. You must give most, if not all, the motifs a twist. Find fresh ways of fulfilling their expectations. In a rom-com, you must find a way to make the romantic couple different. Discover surprising ways to keep them apart. Give them unusual inner issues. Find a new way for them to meet, an unconventional setting, etc.

The movie *Silver Linings Playbook* gained much freshness by developing a story and characters which dealt with mental health. The TV comedy series *Catastrophe* similarly found fresh humour in an unusual couple inadvertently flung together by an unplanned pregnancy. The feature documentary *Twenty Feet from Stardom* took a new angle on celebrity by looking at the backing singers whose voices have been heard on the most successful songs but whose faces and names remain unknown.

Ask yourself what is fresh and surprising about your story – or what could be.

RULE OF THUMB 4

One common way to bring freshness to a story is by combining two different genres. It's unusual for a film to focus on only one genre. Single-genre movies do exist, but they tend to have a deliberately old-fashioned, even retro, feel. Films such as *The Untouchables* – a classic gangster movie about the trapping of Al Capone made by Brian De Palma as an homage to the gangster movies of the past. Similarly, Todd Haynes' 2002 drama of interracial love, *Far from Heaven*, overtly channels the classic 1950s melodramas of directors such as Douglas Sirk.

The same applies to TV, although TV audiences seem to be more tolerant of single-genre stories, especially when it comes to much-loved genres such as crime. A series such as *Midsomer Murders* is an unashamed detective series, delivering unchallenging murder mysteries for entertainment.

For the most part, however, there will be two primary genres in any story. Indeed, almost any genre combination is possible – from Western/survivalist (*The Revenant*) and crime/drama (*Happy Valley*) to action/documentary (*Touching the Void*).

However, be aware that now *both* genres need to run at full value. So, if your TV series is a sports-sci-fi, your story can't get away with

50 per cent sports and 50 per cent sci-fi, but must be 100 per cent sports and 100 per cent sci-fi from start to finish.

There will certainly be other emotions, moods and genres that are important to your story, but that doesn't mean you have to put them all in your pitch. Take Quentin Tarantino's *The Hateful Eight*. This has strong elements of Western, epic, satire, noir, historical and parody. But you'll confuse and annoy your listeners if you throw all these into the pitch. Choose whichever feels strongest (in this case, probably Western/noir).

RULE OF THUMB 5

The premise of your story should reflect the genres it belongs to. There should be something essentially funny about a good comedy pitch; something essentially horrifying about a good horror pitch. Something both comic and horrific in a comedy-horror.

The idea of an actor pretending to be a woman to get a job on a soap opera (*Tootsie*) is intrinsically comic. The idea of a desperate, second-rate thief trying to build a career out of filming the scenes of gruesome car accidents and murders (*Nightcrawler*) is dark and seamy – the essential emotions of a noir.

You don't have to be a stand-up comic to pitch a comedy, but you should allow the humour in the idea to come through your words. Similarly, the words you use in a horror pitch should leave us feeling chilled, a thriller pitch should leave us with a sense of fear, and so on.

....

EXERCISE – **GENRE RESEARCH**

If you've chosen the right person to pitch to, he will be expert in your genres. You need to be as knowledgeable. Be prepared to be questioned on all the typical issues that arise.

Start by hiring or downloading all the relevant films and programmes you can find. This should be fun. It's very unlikely you'll want to write a movie in a genre that you don't enjoy (and even less likely that you'll succeed). Study them closely – the classics and the most recent – to tease out what makes them tick. Make notes about the emotions they bring out, the motifs they use and how they succeed (or fail) to find fresh variations. Buy or download the scripts where possible.

Ideally, you should know most of, if not all, the major films or programmes in your genres, although it's always possible a producer will mention a title you haven't heard of. This is one of the reasons to practise widely before you start pitching to your most serious prospects. If someone comes up with something you've not yet seen, ask them for more details and make a note to watch it as soon as possible.

Read books and articles on your chosen genre but be aware that the vast majority are written from the perspective of film studies. In other words, they are looking from the other end of the telescope – at the finished product. Nevertheless, they are still very useful sources of research. At the very least they give you an audience perspective, and lists of titles to watch.

When it comes to books on genre for writers, there are remarkably few. The best is still *Alternative Scriptwriting* by Ken Dancyger and Jeff Rush (see the bibliography at the end of this book). Kamera Books (the publishers of this book) are so far about the only imprint to publish books on writing for specific genres: www.kamerabooks.co.uk.

....

GENRE TRAPS

There are many genres and subgenres, each with their own characteristic emotions and motifs. Some can be tricky to pitch and you'll need to be aware of the potential pitfalls that lie in wait. Here's a brief checklist of some of the most dangerous genre traps you may find yourself dealing with.

THRILLER

Primary emotion – fear. A thriller always builds on other genres, usually horror, crime or noir, adding a high level of suspense. Don't confuse this with tension. All films should have some kind of tension – in a thriller this becomes full-blooded, non-stop fear.

The biggest trap for the writer is that the pitch fails to create a convincing sense of that necessary fear. Usually, this is because the reasons for the protagonist being in jeopardy are not credible enough. The other typical problem comes from taking five minutes to explain why he's in this mess in the first place. You don't have five minutes; you have a sentence – you must be totally ruthless in cutting your set-up to a few short words.

COMEDY

Primary emotion – laughter. As I said above, the primary trap here is not having a comic premise. It's simply not good enough to say, 'Funny things happen.' Ask yourself what is essentially funny about the situation, the characters or their goals.

SCREWBALL COMEDY

This is a high-energy comedy in which the protagonist is forced to confront his flaws by a screwball character, who crashes into his life and causes mayhem. In the earliest "screwball" comedies, the protagonist was an inhibited man and the screwball a woman whose accident-prone behaviour broke through his protective armour and brought him out of himself. More recent examples have found fresh variations. In *Overboard*, for example, Joanna is a spoilt heiress with amnesia and the screwball character a carpenter she cheated, who takes revenge by claiming she's his wife and getting her to slave for him and his four impossible sons.

A common mistake with screwball is making the screwball character the protagonist. However, the protagonist should generally be the one who undergoes the greatest inner journey (see 'The Inner Story') and a screwball character is more of a force of nature than a character who can change.

If the screwball is the protagonist, then your genre is probably not screwball but...

SATIRE

Also a high-energy genre, satire finds its comedy in characters who are stuck in their flaws and never change. The challenge with pitching satire is finding a story which will provide the intensity that the genre needs to overcome the lack of a character journey.

DRAMA

Drama is the catch-all for stories that don't fall into any of the other genres. Stories without (on the whole) guns, fast cars, spaceships, footballs or ghosts and which are worked out between human beings on a social level. Dramas are resolved through social interaction – usually dialogue – not shooting each other or winning a trophy.

The emotion in a drama is one of sympathy. Note, this is not the same as empathy (which you find in any good fiction story). We may empathise with Joanna, the entitled heiress in *Overboard*, but we don't necessarily sympathise with her.

In a drama pitch you need to ensure we actively sympathise. This is usually because the protagonist is likeable – almost always attractive and intelligent – and is alone, pitted against the power structures of the society around. All their attractiveness and intelligence is of no use to them now. We sympathise with the four adult children in the Danish series *The Legacy* when the unexpected death of their celebrated artist mother turns their lives upside down. Or with the lonely, widowed office worker and the neglected wife in the Indian drama *The Lunchbox* who are thrown together by an accident of fate.

Drama includes many subgenres with drama in the title, such as legal drama, historical drama, political drama, financial drama, medical drama, therapy drama, drama drama (putting on a play), as well as road movie, rite of passage and coming of age.

RITE OF PASSAGE

A subgenre of drama, rite of passage tells the story of a character who is stuck at some phase of life and needs to grow up. The best known subset of rite of passage is coming of age, which deals with puberty and becoming an adult. However, rite of passage stories can occur at any point in life from birth to death, including becoming a teenager, getting your first job, getting married, becoming a parent, retiring, being bereaved and facing terminal illness.

The focus of the story is on the character's inner growth – or failure to grow. The central question (and tension) of the story is about what kind of person the protagonist will become. He has few if any role models to follow and must find his own way.

Confusion often arises when planning such a pitch, because most genres include a journey of growth. However, just because there is an inner journey doesn't mean you have a rite of passage story.

There are two tests as to whether you are right to call yours a rite of passage. The first is that the audience is mostly worried about the inner story. In a crime story, for example, the detective may well grow and learn, but the focus is whether she catches the criminal. In a rite of passage, we don't really care that much about the outer goal. In the movie *Stand by Me*, four boys search for a dead body in a forest, but it's fair to say that the audience doesn't care as much about whether they find it as whether – and how – they grow up.

The second test is to look at the motifs in the story. A rite of passage story is primarily about the passing of time, so there will be many symbols and rites relating to time in the story. Very often, a death acts as a spur to the protagonist early in the story, rattling her equilibrium. There may also be births, christenings, birthdays, barmitzvahs, weddings and so forth.

If your story passes both tests, you can be fairly sure you have a rite of passage script.

COMEDY-DRAMA (SOMETIMES SHORTENED TO DRAMEDY)

This genre double catches many writers out. A true comedy-drama is 100 per cent comedy *and* 100 per cent drama.

Don't be confused by the fact that most dramas have their humorous moments. Some witty dialogue. A few moments of comic relief to lighten the story. You won't fall into the trap if you apply Rule of Thumb 3. The question is: does the audience expect to be both laughing and sympathetic almost all the time. If so, it is a true comedy-drama.

If not, call it a comedy – or drama.

CRIME

If there's a crime in your story, then it's quite likely that at least one of your genres is crime (which covers both detective and gangster). The primary emotion in crime is a feeling of injustice and a desire for justice to be restored.

The problem with crime stories is ensuring we care about the protagonist. If your central character is a professional criminal, we may find it difficult to identify with his goals. If a professional detective, then solving crimes is her job, and so we may need to be given a stronger reason why we should identify with her problems. One common technique is to give the goal a personal edge, such as a link to a previous event, an injustice, a personal involvement with the crime.

NOIR

A genre that writers often forget about when pitching is noir. If the criminal protagonist is an amateur, rather than a professional, criminal then the genre is most likely to be noir. The very name 'noir' suggests the primary emotion – one of darkness and tragedy. The problem with noir is establishing a credible reason why this ordinary person should stumble into committing serious crime.

A strong noir protagonist is someone who is already in a dark place, even if he doesn't know it. He is burnt out and has little to live for. (The original noir protagonists were ex-soldiers who had returned from the horrors of the Second World War.)

It is for this reason that he is likely to become obsessed with someone or something he believes will redeem his life – such as love, money or fame. And it's this object of obsession which leads him to crime. If you have a dark story, especially if the protagonist is on the edge, then you are very likely to be pitching a noir.

TRUE STORY

Writers of fiction and documentaries are often attracted to true stories that are full of exciting scenes, important moments and dramatic events. There is something almost irresistible about knowing these actually took place.

However, the harsh fact is that audiences care less about the truth of a story than whether it holds their attention, with characters who interest them. Partly because they are real, true stories are often episodic and lacking in structure. Their central characters turn out to be passive and one-dimensional. Fictional stories are, to quote Alfred Hitchcock, 'life with the dull bits cut out'. The trouble is, when you start cutting into the structure of a true story you can find that you are left with little or no dramatic spine to work with.

It's rare to find a true story that has enough of a dramatic structure to work on screen without having to invent so much that it loses its truth. If you find one, then grab it and pitch it. If it doesn't have a strong dramatic spine and if your subject isn't well known, you may be better off using it to inspire a fictional work and using the freedom that gives you to make the story really work.

TO SUM UP...

When you tell the producer the genre you are instantly doing three things in a very few words:

- You're telling them the emotion that the audience will be feeling.
- You're telling them if it fits with the kind of project they want to make.
- You're priming them for those elements in the pitch that support the genre – for example, if you say it's a comedy you're preparing them to be ready to laugh.

...And you're doing it right up front, so they don't have to wait around and work it all out for themselves. Why would you not want to do all three things?

We've begun to answer *why* people will want to watch your movie or TV show. Next you need to tell the listener *what* it actually is. Starting with the Outer Story.

THE **OUTER** STORY

A novel, poem or song can take place inside someone's head. Elgar's oratorio *The Dream of Gerontius*, and the John Henry Newman poem it's based on, evoke a man's thoughts at death and his soul's journey to Purgatory. Many great works of art deal brilliantly with inner stories – learning to die, learning to live, discovering the meaning of love, etc. However, without an outer story they cannot be dramatised.

By contrast a screen story, whether fiction or documentary, has to be filmed by a camera. It needs to take place primarily in the visible world. Its characters must take actions that we can see, to achieve goals that are real, concrete and tangible.

So, the next thing that the producer is listening for, after the genre, is whether you have a story that works on screen – an **outer story**.

What is an outer story? An outer story must have three things:

- A character who wants something.
- What they want.
- Someone or something they must overcome to get it.

A CHARACTER WHO WANTS SOMETHING

At the centre of every screen story for any medium we find one or more characters who want to achieve something or avoid something. The hero, or protagonist. Most stories will focus on a single protagonist. Some will have two or more. A few will have many protagonists who either all want the same thing (to break into a bank, to escape a monster, to save a village) or all want different things (we'll come back to that later).

For the purpose of the pitch/log line, you only need to tell us the briefest facts about your protagonist – in no more than two or three words. Is she a failed detective, an ambitious banker, a lone yachtswoman, an intelligent recycling bin?

Don't waste pitching time giving your fictional character's name – it doesn't tell us anything important about the story. Indeed, giving the name will be counterproductive. It's said that the brain can only retain around seven chunks of information at a time – fewer if the listener is busy or distracted. A pitchee will have enough to do, remembering the crucial details of your pitch. So you don't want to tax your overworked, hungover development exec with more information than she needs.

Of course, this doesn't apply if your protagonist is famous, such as Aung San Su Kyi or Reggie Kray. Then you must include his or her name, as this is one of the selling points of your package.

Your protagonist will normally be human, but not always. There have been many successful stories throughout history where the protagonist has been an animal, a god, a force of nature or, more recently, a machine. Anyone or anything can be a protagonist as long as he, she or it has a goal.

WHAT THEY WANT

All well-written characters should want something – this is their motivation and brings them to life. Without a goal there is no story. And what they want must be visible and concrete. It's no good to us if all they want is invisible – such as love, redemption or enlightenment. They will doubtless have these needs, too, but these can only be put on screen if we create visible, concrete manifestations of them:

- The person who needs love can, for example, want a particular person.

- Redemption can be focused into winning a particular football trophy.
- The character who seeks enlightenment can set out on a dangerous pilgrimage.

Showing that you understand this is one of the most important jobs of the pitch. One of the biggest mistakes I see in pitches by inexperienced writers is that they fail to focus this outer goal. Sometimes they have only a generalised idea of what the protagonist wants – such as to be rich, or to be happy. These are important, but they are internal and too vague. To develop a story that works, whether fiction or documentary, the writer must focus these wants onto an external goal.

How – exactly – is the protagonist going to try to get rich? By inventing a new kind of mop (*Joy*)? By robbing a jewellery shop (*Rififi*)? By defrauding investors (*Enron: The Smartest Guys in the Room*)? Only when you can tell us the protagonist's specific goal do we know what we're going to see on screen.

PICTURES IN THE MIND

Whatever the goal, it should create pictures in our minds – the more vivid the better. When listening to the pitch we want to be visualising the story. Obviously the pictures will vary with the genre. *Joy*'s mop yields a more comic, offbeat image than *Rififi*'s jewellery heist, but both are eminently visual in their own way. *Enron* is less easily visualised. A pitch for *The Smartest Guys in the Room* would need to evoke the energy, cut-throat nastiness and colourful characters that the documentary will show us.

WHO OR WHAT IS STOPPING THEM?

It's not enough that the protagonist wants something and goes and gets it. This would make for a rather boring story. We need to see him confronted with obstacles to achieving that goal. Indeed, the story *is* his struggle to overcome those obstacles.

In the outer story, the obstacles must be outer obstacles – people and objects that we can see and film. In the next chapter we'll be looking at his inner obstacles – his fears, distractions, doubts, etc. These will be important, but they don't help you create your outer story. Just as with outer goals, your protagonist must be confronted with outer obstacles that are visible and concrete and outside him.

In the majority of films and TV dramas, his primary obstacles will be other characters. They will oppose him – because they want something different, because they don't like him, don't believe in him or don't trust him, or for myriad other reasons. Most often, there will be a principal antagonist who will lead this opposition. At other times, there may be a group – bandits, the police, the music business, the opposing football team.

There may also be physical obstacles – a desert to cross, a prison to break out of, a spaceship to mend. These are all important because they raise the tension, and force the protagonist to dig deeper into his inner resources to achieve his goal.

When constructing your log line, you may specifically mention a primary obstacle or let it be implied. For example, in a gangster movie you may mention the police chief who's made it his life's work to capture the central character. However, you might prefer to focus on his attempts to avoid capture without going into detail on who it is who's trying to catch him. There's no hard and fast rule and each pitch will have different needs.

WHAT'S AT STAKE?

The protagonist must want something important. In many stories, the hero's life will be at stake – escaping from the dinosaurs, destroying the homicidal robot, surviving the serial killer.

In others, the stakes are more important than life itself. A detective may put his life on the line to save a child from being abused. Failing, but staying alive, would be worse for him than dying. In *Romeo and Juliet* living without each other would be worse than death. They prefer, in the end, to die together than live on alone.

However, when pitching, it may not be obvious to the listener why the stakes are so high. Why is it so important that the two lovers should be together? A good pitch should make the point that Romeo and Juliet are fighting against an unjust social order that divides their families, and are the potential means of healing it.

In most love stories the two lovers also have something in their characters that the other one needs to complete them. It's interesting, in this light, to compare the novel and film adaptation of *Captain Corelli's Mandolin*. In the novel, Corelli is a passionate mandolin player who falls in love with Pelagia, the daughter of a doctor. He admires her scientific intelligence while bringing her an artistic sensibility she needs in her turn. Together they become a complete whole. Apart, they are each lacking. However, unlike the book, the film fails to properly bring this out. Missing this crucial element, many reviews of the movie found the romance unbelievable and the story uninvolving.

This applies across all genres. Why should I care that Anne Visage wins the French presidency in the French political series *Spin* (*Les Hommes de l'ombre*)? Why should I care that Cilla Black, Ray Charles or Tina Turner become successful singers? What would be lost? Maybe they have a unique vision, something that no one else can bring to the world. Or must overcome poverty, disability and abuse. Maybe they have a vital message to convey to the world.

In a few stories, the object of desire may be quite trivial – or even one we don't agree with – but what makes it important is the enormous effort and emotional weight the protagonist places on it.

In *After Hours*, Paul Hackett's goal is simply to get home. What seems a simple aim, with little at stake, becomes more and more dangerous as misadventure piles on misadventure over a single night.

By contrast, the audience is unlikely to sympathise with the central goal in the satirical movie *Wag the Dog*. The US Government wants to conceal the president's advances to an underage girl by inventing a non-existent war with Albania. However, we are sucked into the story because of the way the risks grow for film producer Stanley Motss, as he is increasingly drawn into their plot.

FINDING THE MOST SPECIFIC OUTER GOAL

Problems often occur in locating the protagonist's best outer goal. Remember the outer goal must be visible, concrete, in the real world and specific. But protagonists often have many goals in succession as the story unfolds and it may not always be obvious at first which is going to best serve your pitch.

As a case study, take this outline for an imaginary offbeat comedy-drama:

Harry Thorn, a self-effacing and introverted student, just wants to be happy completing his physics degree, but his family hits hard times and only he can save them from financial ruin. He sets out to find a job, but nothing works out. Running out of options, he realises he must step up and try to rescue the failing family business, which makes crockery. He decides that the only way forward is to enter the business for a design competition. To do this, Harry must enlist the help of a brilliant publicist, a woman he fell out with before he left for college, improve their design team, ramp up production and finally get their newly created plates to Stoke-on-Trent in time to beat the deadline. In the process, he comes out of his shell and learns he can be a leader. Finally, they win first prize and the business is saved.

There are a dozen outer goals here, so which is the most useful for us?

I hope it's obvious to you now that the first, wanting to be happy, is an inner goal and so can be discarded. *Completing his physics degree* disappears from the story and must therefore be part of the set-up rather than the main drama. *Save the family from ruin* is too vague, as is *find a job*. Is the main goal *rescue the family business*? Better but still rather unspecific. But, wait, the story seems to be focusing on the design competition. Is the key goal going to be *enlist a brilliant publicist*? Or *improve their design team* or any of the goals that follow? Well, they are all subsidiary goals, which are necessary steps towards the goal of winning first prize.

In short, the key goal must be *to win the design competition.* Everything else is either set-up or part of the fight to win.

So my outer story pitch might run:

It's an offbeat comedy-drama about a student who sets out to save his family's failing pottery business by winning a national crockery competition.

Note how much has been left out of the final log line – the character's name, the degree, the backstory, the brilliant publicist, the design team, even the race to beat the deadline. None of that is relevant to the pitch.

If you're still not sure you've chosen the right outer goal, look at the story's climax. An outer story ending should answer the major story question raised at the start. So, working backwards, if you know the ending, you can work out what the question must have been.

In the imaginary drama above, the story climaxes with winning first prize – therefore, logically, winning the competition must have been the main outer story goal.

THE SPECIAL CASE OF THE RITE OF PASSAGE STORY

Rite of passage stories can be excellent vehicles for writers and directors entering film or TV as their characters are often naturally engaging and their stories very personal. Producers like them because you don't need to cast expensive star actors. Indeed, they often work better with unknown actors in the main roles.

A rite of passage story will focus mostly on the central character's character journey. As a result, it's easy to forget there's an outer story at all. But that doesn't mean it's not vital. As we've seen, every screen story must have an outer story spine. However, in a rite of passage story it won't be the primary interest. Indeed, audiences may hardly remember it. It's like the string in a pearl necklace. Nobody notices the string, but without it the necklace will fall apart.

Juno focuses on the character of Juno, a pregnant schoolgirl. It would be easy to overlook the outer story, but there is one: her outer goal is to give the baby away for adoption.

In *Beasts of No Nation*, Agu has to learn to grow up fast as his country is torn apart. His outer goal is to survive the civil war as a child soldier.

About Schmidt follows the story of Warren Schmidt as he learns to deal with retirement and losing his wife. However, that wouldn't be strong enough on its own. The writers have provided an outer goal to hold the film together – to drive to his daughter's wedding and persuade her not to get married.

Many TV series, such as *Cold Feet*, *Thirtysomething* and *Friends* simply build their outer stories out of the daily problems that arise naturally in life.

If you're pitching a rite of passage story, you may have to look hard to find the outer story 'string'. You may even have to add one to your script. Look for any elements that could form the basis of an outer goal and obstacle. It could be as basic as having to take a journey. Don't worry too much if the outer story feels rather simple or episodic – rite of passage stories often are. But do ensure that those episodes have strong outer stories in their own right.

PUTTING IT TOGETHER

So far our pitch goes:

It's a (genre/genres) about a (protagonist) who wants (visible outer goal with high stakes) but (outer obstacle).

The last two elements can be switched around as appropriate and sometimes the obstacle will be obvious from the context:

*It's an animation action-adventure about a panda who sets out to save the animals of his valley from an evil snow leopard. (*Kung Fu Panda*)*

*It's a noir Western about a bounty hunter and a wannabe sheriff who want to take a murderess to the gallows before she can be rescued by her homicidal gang. (*The Hateful Eight*)*

*It's a documentary about a young man in Spain who tries to convince a family in Texas that he is their long-lost son. (*The Imposter*)*

*Gangster/noir. It's about a high-school chemistry teacher with cancer who sets out to make and sell crystal meth to pay for his treatment. (*Breaking Bad, *pilot episode)*

You'll notice how little is said here. Finding and focusing your outer story takes determination and the refusal to put up with anything less than your best answer. It means being very precise and asking yourself continually whether you've found the best way to describe your hero, the best goal, the best obstacle. It means being ruthless in cutting the story back to its absolute core essential – no subplots, cinematic diversions or asides.

You may find that the outer story, when you reveal it, feels rather bare and lacks a great deal that's in the full script. That's good! There's no earthly way you can put all the subtleties and richness of your screenplay in a single sentence or even two. This doesn't, of course, mean that you should resort to cliché either. Those few words must be the best and truest you can find. Beware of stereotypes and predictable motivations.

A pitch is like a short poem, a haiku even, telling its story in a very few words.

TO SUM UP...

A screen story must have an outer story:

- **Someone must want something.**
- **It must be visible and concrete – in the outer world.**
- **Something or someone needs to be stopping them.**
- **It should be a matter of life and death – or more important than that.**

If you found that focusing on your outer story was a challenge and felt it rather lacked something, the next chapter will restore your faith in your story. For the fact is, it's almost never the outer story that gives us emotional involvement, it's the inner story.

THE **INNER** STORY

The inner story follows the protagonist's character journey – the way she grows and changes. If the main reason we watch movies and TV programmes is for the emotions they bring (genre), the second and equally important reason is for the inner journey.

In most stories, the inner and outer stories are bound together. The protagonist's inner struggle to grow is forced into being by her outer problems and her attempts to achieve her outer goal are complicated by her inner flaws.

Macbeth's primary flaw is his overweening ambition. Not content to accept his just rewards and wait for time to bring him the throne, he allows Lady Macbeth to talk him into killing the king. As a result, he achieves what he wants but at a tragic price. He has the crown but he cannot hold on to it. His character journey is his increasing awareness of the enormity of what he's done. His tragedy is that this awareness comes all too late.

By contrast, Joy's flaw (in the movie *Joy*) is that she believes what people tell her. She allows her family and friends to persuade her that she's not going to succeed, that they know best, that she should leave them to make the important business decisions. As she sets out to make a success of her invention, her outer *want* (to succeed as an inventor) is constantly thwarted by her inner *need* to learn to stand up for herself. Step by step, she grows more confident and begins to trust her instincts – but at the same time the outer problems grow larger and so force her to continue to grow.

If a protagonist overcomes her flaw and grows quickly enough, she'll achieve her outer goal and the story will end happily. If she fails to overcome her flaw, or doesn't do it in time, like Macbeth, the ending will be a tragic one. In *Chinatown*, Jake Gittes' flaw is a fear of trust and intimacy. He's grown a thick shell to protect himself in the job he does as a private detective. However, to solve the case this time and save Evelyn Mulwray he must learn to let down his defences. Eventually he does, but it's too late. At the tragic end, he closes down again, but now he's worse than before; numb with shock, it seems he will probably never open up to anyone again.

In some stories, the protagonist will partially overcome her flaw, but not fully, yielding a bittersweet ending. In the West African coming-of-age film *Beasts of No Nation* the young Agu is brutally enlisted as a child soldier in a civil war. Surrounded by violence, he is both fascinated and repulsed, growing both stronger but at the same time more callous. The film ends on a mixed note – there is hope for his future, it suggests, but the emotional scars remain.

If your outer story is what your script is about, then the inner story is what it's *really* about. It's the theme of your story. The theme of *Macbeth* is the effects of unbridled ambition.

This is what people respond to, and gives a story its universal appeal. Most of us will be unlikely to murder a king – but everyone has been tempted to do the wrong thing to achieve something they dearly want. And everyone has to learn to stand up for themselves and judge who to trust.

You introduce the inner story to your log line by opening with the protagonist's primary flaw or by specifying how she needs to grow:

This is a (genre) about a (flawed) (protagonist) who wants (outer goal).

Then, to finish, you add a coda. This rounds off the inner story with a twist, suggesting how that character growth might progress – a nod towards the end of the character journey. Often there will be a sense of appropriateness or irony to this twist. Thus the final template for the Advanced Pitch Sentence goes:

This is a (genre) about a (flawed) (protagonist) who wants (outer goal) only to find (necessary character change or insight).

For example, in the last chapter my outer story log line for the imaginary pottery story went:

It's an offbeat comedy-drama about a student who sets out to save his family's failing pottery business by winning a national crockery competition.

Adding the inner story, the log line now becomes:

It's an offbeat comedy-drama about a self-effacing, introverted student who sets out to save his family's failing pottery business by winning a national crockery competition, but if he's to succeed he will have to come out of his shell and learn to lead.

Or *Joy*:

A comedy biopic about an over-trusting woman who invents a self-wringing mop and must not only fight the business community, but must learn to stop relying on the misguided advice of her own family and friends.

Or *Macbeth*:

A tragedy about an overambitious general who seizes his chance to win the throne by murdering his king only to realise, too late, the horrific consequences of what he's done.

HOW TO FIND YOUR INNER STORY?

Inner story is a very personal thing. Your character's inner story will inevitably be closely related to your own. You can't write about flaws without sharing them to some degree, otherwise the end product would be academic and sterile. If you're writing about a man who must learn to face his fears, and are yourself afraid of nothing, or cannot honestly face your own fears, then your story won't work. You'll need to have a profound understanding of what it means to have fears and bring it out truthfully in the script. Otherwise your screenplay will end up one-sided.

We've all seen films in which the end was preordained by the beginning. The writer knows all the answers. The hero must marry the woman he loves, rather than the one with the money. The heroine must do the honest thing and walk away from the job she covets. The choices here have been fixed from the start. The dilemma is no real dilemma. There's no life in such writing.

A character's flaws will lead her into difficult dilemmas, but only if you can truthfully see both sides of these dilemmas will you be able to fully engage the audience.

Of course, I'm not saying that if you're writing about a murderer you're a psychopath! I'm saying the greatest writers are able to look inside and find the flaws they share with their characters.

Now, the fact that a good story must draw on the writer's flaws means that the issues in your inner story are going to be very close to home. I believe that this, more than anything else, is what divides the competent writers from the great. A great writer plays a different mental game. She is able to be brave and open up to her inner flaws with more honesty than the rest.

But this can be painful and takes courage. Your unconscious mind will try to protect you. It will try to save you from those important insights, in an understandable desire to keep you happy. Luckily, there are three powerful ways for us to find out what's really going on.

INNER EXERCISE 1 - YOUR FLAWS

What flaws are you currently most aware of in yourself? Write them down, going into as much detail as you can. Be honest – this is just between you and you. Nobody else needs to know. Can you imagine how these flaws might relate to the story you're telling?

Alfred Hitchcock, in his time the world's greatest director of thrillers, was himself constantly tormented by fear. A magazine journalist once told of giving him a lift following an interview. After dropping Hitchcock off in the middle of town, the interviewer looked back through the taxi's window. Hitchcock was still standing beside the road where he'd been left, frozen in panic as the pedestrians and traffic rushed around him. At the height of his career, he was still capable of being paralysed with anxiety. But Hitchcock drew unflinchingly on his fears to create some of the greatest movies ever made.

A related exercise is to ask what flaws annoy you in other people. We are most often irritated when we see in others the very things we dislike or fear in ourselves.

When you've found what flaws concern you most, whether in yourself or in the people around you, you can begin to look inside your main character and you will find those flaws there, too.

INNER EXERCISE 2 - THEME

What issues do you care about? What lights your fire? What makes you excited, angry, fearful? This will be a strong guide as to the kind of inner story you'd be likely to be attracted to.

Shakespeare could only have written *Macbeth* if he cared passionately about the question of ambition – how far we should go to achieve our ends.

Be honest. There are no good or bad issues, and nobody can dictate what you should care about or should not. It doesn't matter if your burning issue is saving the planet or going on a diet. If that's your issue, then it will almost certainly lead you to understand your character's inner flaws.

INNER EXERCISE 3 - ENDING

If you still haven't found your character's primary flaw, then the ending will usually reveal it. As we saw, it's only when your protagonist is able to overcome his flaws (or ultimately fails to do so) that the story ends. So, working backwards as we did with the outer story, we can ask: *what is your protagonist able to do at the end that he wasn't able to do at the start? What will he never do again?*

Once you've found how he's changed, you can logically work out what must have been his inner problem in the first place.

At the end of *Joy*, Joy is finally able to stand up to her family and learn to ignore their advice – this gives us a major lead as to what her journey must have been.

In *Chinatown*, Jake is (briefly) able to be intimate with Evelyn. This leads to him discovering what's really been going on. However, he's left it too late, and the final shooting leaves him bereft and closed off even more than he was before. This would suggest that his initial flaw was mistrustfulness, a fear of opening up.

Inner story – flaw – theme – ending. They are all connected. Find one and you'll find the others.

HAVE YOU FOUND THE REAL FLAW?

Beware of the flaw that isn't a flaw. Some apparent inner flaws are simply external situations. For example, a disability isn't a flaw. This may be obvious in the case of a physical disability, but less obvious when someone has an internal disability, such as autism or clinical depression. These aren't flaws for the purposes of dramatic storytelling; they are unfortunate situations.

A character journey must involve a trait that the character could – theoretically – change themselves, through a shift in attitude, say, or belief. So, if your character can't read or write, you need to find the real flaw. Is there something in his personality that's stopping him learning (fear of being ridiculed, perhaps)?

An autistic character can't change his autism, but he could have a different, inner flaw, such as anger or lack of confidence. In Mark Haddon's novel *The Curious Incident of the Dog in the Night-Time*, Christopher's learning difficulties appear to be on the autistic spectrum, though it's never specified. But this isn't his flaw. It's the situation he has to cope with. His flaw is his fear of facing the world. Throughout the story, he has to battle with and overcome those fears, step by step.

Sometimes the flaw you find may indeed be an inner flaw, but not the true flaw. For example, you may decide your character's flaw is that he likes to steal things. This is certainly an inner flaw, but it limits you. He can't steal things in every scene.

I'd want to dig deeper and ask if there's a flaw beneath the flaw. For example, he may steal things because he feels insecure. This stronger flaw will feed into more of his character and affect the whole story. Finding the deeper flaw will give your pitch more energy and impact.

Defining your inner story is at the very heart of writing and takes all your psychological insight and more. If this takes time, don't be surprised. It's an ongoing process that you will continue to work on from the very start of a screenplay to the very last polished draft. Indeed, I find I'm still learning about my characters' inner lives through production and post-production to the point when the film is finally locked.

WHAT IF MY CHARACTER NEVER CHANGES?

In most cases, you will need to go back to your script and ensure that he does. Find a flaw that you can show him fighting to overcome. Or you can do the reverse. You can find a strength he has at the end and revise the script so that he has to learn it, scene by scene.

However, it's also possible you are working in one of the three kinds of stories which don't have an inner story or character journey at all.

ACTION-ADVENTURE

You could be writing an **Adventure** story. Adventure takes up half of the genre conventionally known as Action-Adventure. The primary emotion of action-adventure is one of thrills and spills – an action-adventure is a roller-coaster ride of almost non-stop action and it breaks into two subgenres.

In the **Action** half of the genre, the central character does have an inner story, although most screen time is devoted to the action thrills of the outer plot. As a result, action movies tend towards a less complicated character journey.

This doesn't mean that action movies can't be as subtle and insightful as any other genre. The genre includes some of the greats of world cinema, such as Kurosawa's *Seven Samurai*. In this action-epic, seven masterless samurai are hired by peasants to save their village from bandits. As the story progresses, they slowly learn not to look down on the peasants. At the end, those who survive realise that they, the heroes, are in fact the losers, discarded the moment they are no longer needed. The contrast between the happy, singing farmers and the few remaining samurai – condemned to a future without family or roots – is simply sketched out in the final scene, but is no less moving for all that.

On the other side of the hyphen, however, we find **Adventure** stories. These provide no inner story at all; movies such as the Indiana Jones films, or most of the James Bond franchise. We, the audience, don't expect Indiana to spend the movie facing his deep inner personality flaws. He has flaws, certainly, such as his fear of snakes – but no one expects him to undergo any serious inner change.

Interestingly, when the producers tried to introduce a character journey for James Bond, in *The Living Daylights* and *Licence to Kill*, the audience and critics didn't like it at all. Subsequent Bond movies, such as *Skyfall* and *Spectre*, have allowed him to have flaws but abandoned any attempt to make him try to overcome them.

To compensate for the lack of that crucial inner story, adventure stories need to provide the audience with something that will compensate them – exotic locations, rapidly moving plots, visual fun and high-intensity, roller-coaster action.

A TV series such as *Spooks* (titled *MI-5* in the US and Canada) works in a similar way, allowing for the constraints of a lower budget. It's a spy-adventure series about a special high-tech unit dedicated to protecting Britain from attack from all over the world, a log line which promises energetic, high-stakes stories and a fast pace.

SATIRE

The second genre which offers no inner journey, **Satire** is a very savage form of comedy, which gains its force from the fact that its characters will never change. They are stuck firmly in their flaws and that's why we laugh.

A satire such as *The Big Short* presents us with a cast of bankers, hedge-fund managers and investors whose individual greed, complacency and manipulativeness are fixed. These are not people who will learn and grow. Nor would we expect them to.

As with adventure movies, the lack of an inner story needs to be compensated for with a high level of energy, in this case vividly drawn, forceful characters trying to make the most money out of a situation that we all know is headed for disaster.

Thirdly, **Series** and **Multi-stranded Stories** may or may not have inner stories and, when they do, they often bring very special demands, as we'll see in the next chapter.

TO SUM UP...

- **Your strongest pitch will combine the genre with your outer and inner stories.**
- **It will tell the listener the protagonist's flaw and how they need to grow.**
- **Your characters' flaws may not be easy to define.**
- **Inner story, flaw, theme, ending – find one and it will lead to the rest.**
- **Adventure stories and satires offer no character change, so must provide a high-energy premise to compensate.**

SERIES AND MULTI-STRANDED FILMS

Pitching a TV series is trickier than pitching a single movie or TV drama. What the producer needs to know is whether your series has 'legs' – in other words, if there is enough story potential in your material to justify the extra cost that the length will entail. Holding an audience for the length of a single movie or drama is hard enough. Ensuring they return week after week is a much tougher prospect. And yet writers do it all the time.

There are two kinds of series. The first comprises a single story broken into parts; the second features a different story in each episode.

SERIAL/MINI-SERIES

In the UK a single story series will often be called a **Serial** (**Mini-Series** in the US). Most classic TV adaptations are serials/mini-series – from *Bleak House* and *War and Peace* to *House of Cards*. Original serials such as *The Bridge*, *Unforgotten* and *Deutschland83* fall into the same category.

Pitching a serial is the simpler of the two. You only have one story to deal with – so your pitch will more or less be the same form as a single drama. However, your pitch needs to be strong enough to convince the producer that the story works over a number of parts. This means building up the intensity of the situation, the stakes and the strength of the central character.

A pitch for the British TV crime serial *Unforgotten* might go: *A skeleton is discovered on a London building site and turns out to be that of a mixed-race man killed almost 40 years earlier. The investigation that follows over six episodes opens up the hidden secrets of four seemingly unconnected people who have since gone their separate ways.*

The initial discovery sets up the mystery that will drive the plot. The second sentence introduces the 'legs' – four characters with something to hide.

With the German series *Deutschland83* you could start: *It's an eight-part spy-thriller set during the Cold War, in which an idealistic East German border guard is forced to work undercover in the West German army to steal NATO plans for nuclear war.*

This set-up establishes high stakes. To show it's not simply a single drama story, I'd want to use my second sentence to bring out the material for continually ratcheting up the tension, while developing the protagonist's character arc:

Everything here is different, nothing is what it seems and he soon learns that his ideals will not protect him.

EPISODIC SERIES

The second kind of series, an **Episodic Series**, comprises individual stories, each episode standing more or less alone. A sitcom such as *Episodes* or *Parks and Recreation* or a crime series such as *Midsomer Murders* or *Poirot* sets up a framework within which different stories will play out each week, focusing mostly on the same main characters. Unlike a one-off drama or a serial, there's no character journey between episodes. Indeed, except possibly for the first and last, the stories could probably be shown in any order.

Gregory House doesn't find his touchy-feely side by the end of *House*. If there is a moment of enlightenment and growth – if, for example, Harold Steptoe realises that he must leave and strike out on his own without his father at the end of an episode of *Steptoe and Son* – you can be sure that the moment will pass, and he'll fall back into his old flaws yet again, the tragedy of his failure made palatable, indeed enjoyable, by the quality of insight and humour.

What is more important for an episodic series pitch is the constellation of characters who will bump into each other week after week.

HYBRID SERIES

Increasingly we're seeing the growth in TV of what I call the **Hybrid Series** – such as *The West Wing* or *The Good Wife*. In a hybrid series there is an ongoing story as well as an individual episode story. So, for example, in *The Good Wife*, we follow the overarching story of Alicia Florrick's fight to re-establish herself as a lawyer after her husband is sent to jail for corruption, while each individual episode brings her a new case to fight.

As with a pitch for a serial, a pitch for an episodic or hybrid series has two jobs to do – you have to pitch the overall series concept in a sentence (or two). Then you follow with examples of one or more episodes, each with its own one/two-sentence log line.

Let's look at the overall series log line first.

As with single story films and dramas, the heart of your pitch lies in the central character, his goals and flaws. The difference is that a series draws its dramatic energy from a small cast of recurring characters, whose flaws and antagonisms will catch fire week after week.

Each episode of *Dad's Army* brings us the bumptious Captain Mainwaring, the lackadaisical Sergeant Wilson, panicky Corporal Jones, inept and naive Pike, the officious ARP Warden Hodges, and Walker, the black-market spiv. Each character irritates, annoys and generally treads on the toes of all the others. This internal bickering is what powers the whole series.

Similarly, the variously ambitious, driven, energetic, vain, naive and idealistic characters provide the dramatic fuel at the heart of *The West Wing*.

So, your series log lines might go:

It's a sitcom set in the Second World War about an inept but well-meaning troop of Home Guard volunteers whose vanities, fears and bickerings constantly threaten to sabotage their plans to defend their small seaside town from imminent invasion.

It's a political drama series about the many clever and flawed people who run the West Wing of the White House, their ambitions, feuds, ideals and struggles to do their best for their country, or simply to survive another day in the bear pit that is Washington, D.C.

THE EPISODE PITCH

So far, we've shown the producer the overall concept – but not how it will play out in practice. You need to give her at least one example of an episode, and the best way to do this is to go back to the standard template – genre, flawed protagonist, goal... Or in the words of comedy writer Paul Bassett Davies, 'In walks a problem.'

The simplest way to lead into this is: *For instance...*

*For instance, one week the bumptious Captain Mainwaring grows convinced that the Nazis could attack at any moment. But he needs weapons, so he decides to requisition historic army weapons from the local museum. However, to do this he must outwit the curator, Lance Corporal Jones's father. (*Dad's Army: *'Museum Piece')*

*For instance, in one episode, the leak of a damaging internal memo accusing the president of being too timid sparks a desperate search for the anonymous writer but also a furious argument among the staff as to whether the writer might indeed be right. (*The West Wing: *'Let Bartlet be Bartlet')*

In the UK, series are generally commissioned to run for between six and thirteen episodes. In the US, commissions of 26 episodes are not unknown. Either way, you'll need to convince your producer that you can come up with enough problems with enough variation between them that you won't be repeating the same story each time.

To do that you'll pitch one or two examples up front, but you'll also need to have at least half a dozen log lines for further episodes, ready to bring out when asked.

Note, you won't be expected to have scripts for more than the pilot episode. But you will need to have clear ideas about the rest of the series and be ready to talk about them in the pitch meeting.

MULTIPLE PROTAGONIST AND MULTIPLE-STRAND STORIES

The majority of screen stories and many TV series and serials revolve around a single protagonist; however, many will feature two or more equally important protagonists. Films such as *Thelma and Louise*, *Ocean's Eleven*, *Jules et Jim* and *Babel*, documentaries such as *Touching the Void* and *One Day in September* and series like *The Bridge*, *Humans* or *Friends*. How should we pitch these?

The first step is to work out which kind of multiple protagonist story we're dealing with. As with series and serials, there are two sorts – stories in which all the protagonists want the same goal and stories in which they are all pursuing different goals.

In the movies *Thelma and Louise*, *Ocean's Eleven* and the Scandinoir TV series *The Bridge* the protagonists want the same thing. Thelma Dickinson and Louise Sawyer are both trying to run from the FBI. The gang in *Ocean's Eleven* are united in their aim of robbing three casinos at once. The two cops at the centre of *The Bridge* both want to solve the same crime.

MULTIPLE PROTAGONISTS – SINGLE GOAL

If the protagonists share the same outer goal, you start developing your log line as you would with a single protagonist – focus first on that shared goal.

Two women go on the run...
A gang of thieves set out to rob...

However, they are most unlikely to share the same flaws. In a well-constructed story, the protagonists should always be different from each other, with different inner issues. So, to complete the log line, you must stand back and see what their individual character journeys have in common.

So, in *Seven Samurai*, each of the samurai comes with his personal strengths and weaknesses – one is cold and detached, one committed but angry. However, each in his own way reflects the tragic isolation of the masterless samurai, doomed always to be rejected by the lowly peasants whose simple life they will never be able to take part in themselves.

In many dual-protagonist stories, their flaws may be opposite yet related. Louise is headstrong while Thelma is more passive and conventional. Pitching for *Thelma and Louise*, you might add how they learn from each other. Thelma learns from Louise to be more self-reliant while Louise learns to face up to her own past.

There is no significant inner story in *Ocean's Eleven* as it's primarily an adventure movie – a caper story whose attraction comes from the many twists and turns of the plot as the gang attempt to do what is apparently impossible. In pitching a story like this, I'd focus on the size of the obstacle, robbing three highly protected casinos at the same time, and the motivations: that the robberies are planned as an elaborate revenge for events that took place years before.

MULTIPLE PROTAGONISTS – MULTIPLE GOALS

Then there are stories whose protagonists each have entirely different goals, and sometimes different storylines entirely. Multi-stranded films such as *Nashville* or Paul Haggis's *Crash* or multi-stranded mini-series such as *Humans* or *War and Peace*.

Here your task is very similar to pitching an episodic series. You must step back and see what it is that all those goals and storylines have in common. Why are they all in the same story together? There will invariably be something that unites them – it will probably be connected with the theme or even the characters' inner stories.

So, in *Crash* all the stories are variations on coping with racism for people who live in Los Angeles.

Nashville tells the interlocking stories of a group of people who are trying to use the country music business to their own ends.

War and Peace could be said to be about young people in Tsarist Russia trying to find love and fulfilment at a time when their homeland is under threat.

The series *Humans* is about different people – and robots – each grappling in their different ways with what it means to be human and what it means to be a machine.

You would then probably need to give an example or two of the key characters or plot strands, just as you would with an episodic series, developing a log line for each:

> *For instance, a black businessman who's afraid to rock the boat fights to save his marriage after he fails to protect his wife from a racist cop...* (Crash)

> *For example, when Joe buys an attractive female robot without consulting his family, each of the family members has to readjust to the new arrival. His wife feels she's being replaced, their youngest daughter becomes dangerously attached to her, and the robot herself begins to reveal she has her own issues to resolve...* (Humans)

TO SUM UP...

- A serial/mini-series follows a single story across multiple parts.
- Pitch as you would a single story movie or drama but show it has 'legs'.
- Pitch a series by giving the overarching idea and then a sample episode.
- With multiple-protagonist stories see if the protagonists share the same outer goal.
- If there is a single goal, pitch the shared outer goal and look for what their inner journeys have in common.
- If they have different goals, pitch as you would a series.

PITCHING **DOCUMENTARY**

For the most part, pitching a single documentary or documentary series will be very similar to pitching a fiction project. In the words of award-winning documentary writer-director Ulrike Kubatta, 'Almost always, it still boils down to "What is the story?" The log line.' Indeed, I've included a number of documentary pitches in previous chapters. However, there are a few significant differences you need to be aware of.

DOCUMENTARY GENRES

Just as with fiction, you do best to start with your genre. Many fiction genres are appropriate to documentary, such as crime (*The Murder Detectives*, *The Thin Blue Line*), sports (*Senna*), action (*Touching the Void*, *One Day in September*), War (*The Great War*, *Shoah*) and biopic (*Amy*, *Twenty Feet from Stardom*, *Finding Vivian Maier*). And the same genre rules apply – you need to know the genre motifs and yet supply them in a fresh and different manner.

However, there are additional forms which are more common in documentary than in fiction, such as **educational** (which includes **science documentaries**, **arts documentaries**, **historical**, etc.) and **investigative documentary**.

Reality has become such a popular documentary genre that it is hard at the time of writing to find interest from TV channels for any other kind, unless the filmmaker can provide an extremely compelling pitch. It grew out of the success of reality game shows such as *Big Brother* and the *Idols – Pop Idol, American Idol*, etc.

With reality documentary, in its different forms, the filmmaker creates a situation and then follows it, for example, arranging for people to experience a very different life from the one they're used to (*Undercover Boss*), swap places (*Wife Swap*) or learn a new skill in a short period of time (*Faking It*).

In the series *The Secret Millionaire*, a millionaire goes undercover to watch and work with a group of deserving volunteers or charity workers. At the end of each programme the secret millionaires reveal who they really are and decide whether to make significant donations of money.

Variations include following a problem solver as he or she goes round helping those in need (*Obsessive Compulsive Cleaners*, *Supernanny*, *The Dog Whisperer*).

Obviously, as with fiction, two genres often combine – for example, an investigative documentary which centres on a crime or an educational documentary which tells the story of the Second World War.

OUTER AND INNER STORIES

Having established the genre, you develop the inner and outer stories in exactly the same way we saw earlier. 'When pitching it's easy to get lost in the characters and the style,' says Kubatta. 'You have to have a clear conflict and an expected outcome. A goal that's being aimed for, or a big change.'

You can focus this aim and raise the stakes by adding a crucial deadline such as a competition. Thus, for example, a possible log line for the documentary reality series *Faking It* would be:

> *A member of the public has just four weeks to learn a new skill, before competing against experienced practitioners. They must then see if they can fool a team of experts who will try to judge which of the competitors is the 'fake'.*

As with a fiction series pitch, you would then give examples of possible episodes, to bring the idea to life and show it has legs:

For instance, we'll see a classical cellist who's always wanted to be a club DJ, there's a burger-van proprietor who's going to train with Gordon Ramsay to become a cordon bleu chef, and a former naval petty officer who's going to see if he can pass as an authentic drag artist. ('Cellist Turns DJ', 'Burger Flipper to Chef' and 'Faking It... as a Drag Artist')

CHARACTER

Your protagonists must grip us as strongly as in a fiction pitch, with a character journey, a flaw to overcome (or a failure to overcome it).

If your story is in the past, you will need to bring out what we will learn about the people involved and how they changed over time. For example, in *Touching the Void*, the filmmakers set out to tell the compelling story of climbers Simon Yates and Joe Simpson. The two men conquered one of the most difficult peaks in the Peruvian Andes only for Simpson to fall off the edge of a cliff leaving Yates to make an agonising decision. The only way he could save himself was by cutting the rope that linked him to his friend, condemning Simpson to an almost certain death.

The viewer doesn't know the outcome till the very end. Meanwhile, in exploring the characters of Yates and Simpson, along with their inexperienced base-camp assistant, Richard Hawking, the documentary team had three characters whose fears and dilemmas could maintain the tension throughout.

If the story hasn't yet taken place, you need to show that you have chosen strong protagonists who will come to life on the screen.

For example, in *The Secret Millionaire*, the filmmakers were careful to select men and women who had a personal story to tell, often self-made, and to put them in situations which forced them to confront their inner issues. In addition, the volunteers and charity workers they met also had a strong backstory, interesting lives and compelling goals of their own.

In *Faking It*, the protagonists were chosen for their screen presence but also the appropriateness and difficulty of the skill they had decided to learn. Essential to the concept was surrounding the 'faker' with experienced trainers who could give their best advice, but had to watch helplessly as the central characters of each episode struggled with their problems, had to face their worst fears and often almost gave up before the final test.

PUTTING YOUR STORY ON THE SCREEN

One major difference from fiction is the importance of showing how you intend to make your documentary work on screen. With a fiction pitch, the producer will be less concerned with how the story will be made and much more with the essence of the story and characters – and ultimately the script. With a documentary, however, there is no detailed script, and far less freedom to invent for the camera. As a result, how you intend to film your documentary becomes critical.

There are a number of possible approaches, which can be used in a variety of combinations:

- **Talking head** – interviews with experts, participants, etc. This is a popular fallback for would-be documentary makers, but often hated by producers who believe (not without cause) that it leads to static and flat filmmaking. It can work, with an absolutely captivating interviewee, but more often it will kill your pitch stone dead, so be careful.

- **Presenter-led** – very popular at the moment, especially if you have a celebrity presenter. Of course, they should be right for the subject and you'll need at least a letter of intent from the celebrity concerned.

- **Archive footage** – can be a useful way of bringing an old story to life, if you can get it, but it needs to be good.

- **Live footage** – often the best way, but you need to be able to convince the producer that you'll be able to deliver the goods (see 'Access' below).

- **Secret filming** – a version of live footage where the participants don't know they're being filmed. Can produce great results, though check in advance that you are legally able to use what you get. It may also involve putting the people doing the filming in a certain amount of danger. Are you and they prepared for that?

Other key styles include:

OBSERVATIONAL/FLY ON THE WALL

In an observational or fly-on-the-wall approach, the camera is as objective as possible. Often the programme will be shot from fixed or remotely controlled cameras – such as *24 Hours in A&E* where over 70 cameras follow every moment of a single day in the Accident and Emergency ward of a major city hospital. Alternatively, there may be a camera team, but it will remain unobtrusive and attempt to record events without comment or bias. In extreme versions, there is no commentary and no music.

Of course, a totally unbiased approach is never entirely possible as there are always decisions to be made by the filmmakers regarding choice of subject, camera placement and editing. But the aim is for a sense of detached observation of reality.

The style is common in TV but far less so in cinema, partly because of cost, demanding a high ratio of shot material to final programme. A rare recent example is *National Gallery* shot by the veteran Frederick Wiseman. Running three hours, it follows staff and visitors to the gallery over many weeks, with deadpan editing and no voiceover, title cards or graphics, a style which Wiseman has more or less patented over the years.

PARTICIPATORY/REFLEXIVE (INCLUDING FIRST PERSON)/AUTHORED

Also sometimes known as **performative**, this style of documentary could hardly be more different from observational. A **participatory** documentary foregrounds the making of the film. The filmmaker will normally be highly visible and/or audible. The implication is that you can never truly present the unvarnished truth and the very making of a documentary changes what is being filmed.

Examples include documentaries by Louis Theroux, in which the very search for truth by the presenter/filmmaker becomes central to the story, and his frustrations and setbacks along the way form the spine of the film.

TYPICAL ISSUES YOUR DOCUMENTARY PITCH WILL NEED TO ADDRESS

In 'What They Want', we saw the five key questions that any producer needs answered. In addition, there are some very specific questions that a documentary-maker needs to address:

DO YOU HAVE ACCESS?

Crucial. Do you have the means to do everything you say you're going to do? Do you have the necessary permissions? Have you found the people you need and do you have their agreement? Do you have permission to film where you will need to? You should have written agreements, ideally contracts, but at the very least letters of agreement.

This includes showing that you have or can get permission to use any copyright material – archive film or stills, poems, music, paintings, etc. You may not have the funds to pay for them, but you should know how much money will be involved and have a provisional agreement that you can use anything you'll need. If you have any doubts over what permissions you'll need you should consult a media lawyer.

WHY NOW?

Many successful documentary pitches create a sense of urgency. As one documentary filmmaker said to me, 'Documentaries are often slaves to time. There's a resistance to historical ideas among commissioning editors. They want contemporary stories – current themes and topical ideas.'

Why is this absolutely the right time to be making this? Does it say something important about today's society? Or take a historical event that has parallels with modern life? Even if you aren't asked the question specifically, you should ensure that you make a strong point about the topical relevance of the story or series when you pitch – whether the subject is social media or Socrates...

When pitching my documentary *Sex, Drugs and Dinner* to the BBC, I had to ensure we covered all these issues. The inspiration for the documentary was when I discovered that at the same time as the West sends food aid to stop famine in poor countries you can buy food exported from those countries in Western supermarkets. What kind of mad system allowed this? This led me into an investigation of the corrupt and self-serving nature of the large organisations that grow and sell food around the world. A system that leaves societies starving and whole countries on the edge of disaster.

However, I wanted to find a fresh way to approach the subject. One that would attract an audience which would not normally watch worthy, environmental doom-and-gloom. I decided that the best way to do this would be through black humour. I pitched the idea to producer Frances Berrigan. She liked the concept and we approached the BBC, casting as our presenter a stand-up comic who was known for his barbed political views – Alexei Sayle.

I also wanted to film people who lived in developing countries, to hear their problems and also to show that they were essentially no different from those in the West. We showed the BBC we had access to them by bringing in the world development charities Oxfam, Christian Aid and CAFOD.

Finally, we underlined how topical this issue was – linking to a major environmental summit that was due to take place in a few months' time. As a result, Alan Yentob, then head of BBC2, cleared a prime-time Saturday night slot and *Sex, Drugs and Dinner* was shot and broadcast in just five months, going on to win an award for best network programme of the year.

In documentaries, as with fiction, you need to have done your homework. Feature documentaries are booming, yet paradoxically the documentary market in general is increasingly demanding. Commissioning editors expect a level of cinematic and narrative excitement that is difficult to deliver, especially on today's lower budgets. And because there is rarely going to be a detailed script, the bar for a documentary pitch is set very high.

TO SUM UP...

- A documentary pitch is fundamentally similar to a fiction pitch.
- Bring out your genre or genres.
- Evoke a strong story.
- Tell the expected outcome, a goal or a significant change.
- The cast of your documentary is a vital part of the pitch.
- Be prepared to talk about how you will put it on the screen.
- Ensure you can get the necessary access and permissions.
- Build a sense of urgency – why now?

WHAT IF?

What we've developed so far is a robust template that will bring you dividends when pitching the vast majority of single stories and series episodes. You will rarely fail with the form – *This is a (genre) about a (flawed) (protagonist) who wants (outer goal) only to find (necessary character change or insight).*

It will work for all kinds of movies, documentaries and single dramas, for series episodes and for any mini-series which follows a single story from beginning to end.

However, if you're having problems boiling your story down to its log line, join the club. The truth is, it's not easy. We all want to hold on to our favourite ideas, to include those clever subplots and twists. You have to be absolutely ruthless if you're to pare down your story to its core.

And patient. Finding the elusive spark your pitch needs doesn't always happen at once. Sometimes, only with determination and after trying it out on many different listeners will it suddenly catch fire.

In this chapter we'll look at some ways you can add to your pitch and some traps to avoid.

MENTAL REAL ESTATE

This is a term coined by Hollywood screenwriters Ted Elliott and Terry Rossio in their blog, *WordPlay*. In an article on Mental Real Estate, Rossio talks about things that are so widely known that they occupy a piece of 'real estate' inside people's brains. In extreme cases, they occupy millions of brains around the world.

Imagine walking into a studio office in 1998 and saying just two words: *Harry Potter*. The first Harry Potter books had already become international bestsellers. Potter merchandising was all round the world. Harry Potter occupied a patch of brain cells, a piece of Mental Real Estate, in millions of heads all around the world. No prizes for guessing a film producer might be interested in tapping into that ready-made market.

But Mental Real Estate is not just about books. Almost any name or idea in the public eye can add audience appeal – whether a famous place, a new technology, a popular idea, a familiar piece of music or a buzz word.

'*Jaws* in space' uses Mental Real Estate twice. First there's the blockbuster movie *Jaws* and then there's 'space' – always popular and particularly so just ten years after the first man reached the moon.

When the internet first hit the public imagination, the classic 1940 rom-com *The Shop Around the Corner* was remade to incorporate email as *You've Got Mail*. The story of *Casablanca* could have taken place in many towns or cities in many different countries, but the name Casablanca has a romance that added to the saleability of the movie.

Mental Real Estate can bring positive resonances to your story. Indie movie *George Washington* has nothing overtly to do with the US president, but is about a group of underprivileged kids who have to deal with a tragic accident – and one of them is called George. But the name can't help but trigger meaningful comparisons between the ideals that helped found the United States and the lives of these teenagers today.

....

EXERCISE

Look for elements of Mental Real Estate that can help trigger audience memories and responses: jobs (*The Negotiator*), iconic buildings and locations (*National Gallery*, *My Beautiful Laundrette*), songs (*Blue Velvet*), works of art (*The Girl with the Pearl Earring*) and more. They may already be there in your script, or they may be easily added without problem. You should also look at:

- Locations – would your story work equally well in a more interesting setting?

- Character names – might a more resonant character name yield a stronger title?

- Character types – can your protagonist have a job or other attribute that's being widely discussed?

- Technology – what are people using that you can include in your pitch? Twitter? Snapchat? What's hot now?

- History – you may not have famous historical figures in your story, but you can name characters, buildings, football teams, etc., after famous people from the past.

....

The possibilities are almost endless. Only, too often, we choose key elements in our stories without really thinking why. Thinking clearly about each choice can only help focus your script.

Don't do anything that spoils or distorts your story, but be open to Mental Real Estate ideas that improve it and give your pitch the extra boost that turns a maybe into a yes.

WHAT IF? – AND OTHER QUESTIONS

Some writers like to develop their pitch by starting with a question – such as 'what if?'

'What if you were getting ready for your 45th wedding anniversary and you learned your husband had always loved someone else?'
(45 Years)

Or:

> *'What if the president of France was killed by a lone protester and his would-be successor invented a terrorist conspiracy to increase his votes?' (Spin – series 1)*

You can use other questions, too.
Could you imagine...?
Did you know...?
Have you ever thought...?

> *'Did you know that for years before the banking crisis of 2008 there were men who warned it would happen – and nobody believed them. So they started placing bets...' (The Big Short)*

> *'Have you seen all these loyal wives of politicians, intelligent and well educated, who stand by their husbands and bury their own careers? Suppose one wife decided to be different...' (The Good Wife)*

> *'Could you believe that a self-effacing nanny who died in poverty is now considered to be one of the master photographers of the twentieth century? And yet nobody knew who she was?' (Finding Vivian Maier)*

> *'Have you ever thought what ducking and diving an ordinary prisoner would need to do to survive in prison? How the best way to keep your dignity is to wake up every morning and look for a way to cheat the system...?' (Porridge)*

Questions like these can make a great set-up for your pitch, laying the emotional ground and engaging the listener's imagination. Most importantly, they are building up the story behind the story – showing that there will be strong publicity angles once the film is made.

Of course, there is the danger that the question becomes so fascinating to the listener that he ends up more interested in finding his own answer than in hearing yours!

Writer-director Naz Sadoughi tells of the dangers that can await if you overdo it:

'A few years ago one of my ideas was shortlisted by Channel 4. I had to go in and pitch to a group of producers and TV executives... I arrived in a bit of a daze – when I walked into the meeting one of the producers asked me how I was and to break the ice I told them about the traumatic incident I'd suffered just the day before. I'd had to rush my unconscious five-year-old daughter to hospital after she knocked herself out and had then ended up being treated for shock myself! My plan worked, the ice was broken and the panel were intrigued and sympathetic, and everyone started to talk about childhood accidents and A&E expeditions... We were all getting on swimmingly and I felt that they'd really warmed to me.

'Then it was time to pitch. It started off OK but by midpoint I'd lost my way. What struck me was that when I arrived I'd recounted my real-life experience very vividly, with so much passion, so that by the time I came to describe the pitch it very quickly began to feel contrived, artificial and less vivid than my personal encounter... I think the executives must have felt it too as I didn't get the job and wonder if it might have been different had I simply pitched my idea without having gone into any personal issues first.'

Make sure the pitch that follows is as compelling as the promise.

YOUR INSPIRATION

This is a stronger and safer version of the 'what if?' opening. It's an excellent way to start, because it establishes you as an essential part of the project while immediately engaging the listener's interest.

Did the idea come from a true story? Or a personal experience? A thought that arrived out of the blue or a character you knew as a child? Did you find yourself growing angry at the treatment of disabled people or fascinated by the idea of a woman falling in love with a condemned murderer? Begin with your moment of inspiration. Draw the producer in with the story of how this script came to be.

The point to be aware of is that you are as important a part of the sales pitch as the story itself. By leading with what inspired you, you highlight your passion and your personal journey in creating it. You're also hinting at how useful you'll be for publicity once the film or drama has been made.

Be careful, however, to keep any introductions short – one to two sentences maximum before you cut straight to your log line. A lengthy set-up is as bad as a lengthy pitch. However good the lead in – you still have to deliver the goods.

TITLE MASH-UP

Once very popular, now far less so, this rams together two unlikely companions in a would-be sexy combination such as:

It's Rambo *meets* Silver Linings Playbook.

Or:

It's The Office *meets* The Sopranos.

A variation might be to give one title plus a twist:

It's Groundhog Day *set on a Mumbai commuter train.*

Be careful with this kind of pitch intro. For one thing, they can sound more alluring to the pitcher than the pitchee. You may also have hit on two movies or TV programmes that the producer absolutely hates.

But most important of all, if you mention any film or programme in your log line it must obey two important rules:

1. It must have gone into profit – otherwise you're telling the listener that your idea is just like one that made a loss.

2. It must have been produced in the last 18 months. The industry moves fast, and anything older than a year and a half has already passed into history. Believe me, if you break that rule someone at some point will say your project sounds dated.

If you really want to mention movies as reference points in a pitch meeting, it's safer to leave it till after you've made your one-sentence pitch. It's fine if you mention favourite old movies and programmes later in the conversation. However, you still want to be a little careful. You don't want to enthuse about how much your thriller series resembles the Icelandic series *Trapped* if it turns out the producer you're pitching to hated it. Worse, that she had a series turned down that was in competition with it!

(It goes without saying that, in a pitch meeting, you should avoid criticising any work *of any kind*. It may not be on her CV, but the person you're talking to may well have worked on the production without credit, or be friends with, married to or having an affair with someone who did!)

CLEVER-CLEVER COMBOS

While we're on the subject of mash-ups, there was once a fashion in the industry to jam a series of clever-sounding ideas together to make something sounding smart and catchy; pitches like:

It's about five dwarfs, three bananas and a dog from Hell.

Personally, I don't like them and thankfully their day has long passed. I don't think I've ever heard one that didn't come over as vacuous, smug and self-satisfied. But that's just my opinion. By all means, have a go, if you think you can create one that actually works. I'm sure one day someone will.

Actually, I'm not sure at all. But then, every rule is there to be broken.

PRACTISE, PRACTISE, PRACTISE

The only sure-fire way to improve your pitch is to keep working on it. Try it out on everyone you know: friends, family, family pets. Blake Snyder, in *Save the Cat*, recommends accosting complete strangers in Starbucks. I don't know I'd go so far, but wholeheartedly support the underlying idea: keep practising your pitch on anyone and everyone who'll listen. Look for that spark that shows your idea is starting to catch fire.

As you develop, you'll find yourself automatically hearing what works and what doesn't, shifting words and phrases on the fly, seeing the reaction in their eyes before they even speak. Under the pressure of pitching to a real person, you'll quite instinctively start to make improvements that you would never do on your own in a room.

Less socially challenging places than Starbucks would be industry networking events, film screenings, writing groups and film clubs. Check, before pitching, that the pitchee doesn't mind being pitched to.

It could even give you a useful answer to the awkward party moment when you tell people you're a screenwriter and they ask, 'What have you done?'

Instead of mumbling something incoherent and resolving never to own up to being a writer again, now you can proudly say, 'I have a script currently in development.' And then you try out your pitch.

TO SUM UP...

- **Mental Real Estate can give you an entry into millions of brains across the planet.**
- **Some pitchers like to begin with a question, but you don't have to.**
- **Title mash-ups can work in the right circumstances; clever-clever combos rarely do.**
- **Practise your pitch on anyone who'll listen (even in coffee shops if you're brave enough).**

COPYRIGHT AND CONFIDENTIALITY

Before we go on, I must deal with the fear many writers have that someone will steal their ideas. In fact, this is not generally an issue for experienced writers, who understand that pitching is a central part of the job and that while ideas do occasionally get stolen, it's extremely rare.

In fact, the problem in most cases is less stopping producers stealing your pitch and more getting them to take notice of it in the first place. In reality, taking your idea without paying for it would be a highly unlikely outcome. For one thing, as we saw earlier, a good pitch is no guarantee of a good screenplay. Why would a producer go to all the expense of hiring another writer, who is going to spend six months to a year developing the script and possibly find it doesn't work, when they can read yours?

If the script works, it will almost invariably be quicker and easier to buy it from you than to commission someone else who may not do such a good job. If it doesn't work, then it's almost always going to be better (and cheaper) to ask you to make the first attempt at redrafting before thinking of bringing in anyone else.

COPYRIGHT PROTECTION

However, this doesn't mean you shouldn't protect yourself. First, there is no copyright in ideas, only the way they are developed. So the more you develop your ideas the better. Any words you have written down will automatically be your copyright under UK law, although the law varies in different countries and you should check out the situation where you live.

Assuming you haven't used anyone else's material, nobody can use it without your permission. You don't even have to put a © symbol on the front page, though you can, next to the date. However, repeating a copyright reminder on every page merely looks amateurish.

This is another reason not to pitch to serious buyers until you have written the script – as a fully developed screenplay is the best protection you can have. However, if you find yourself having to pitch before writing the script, then the more you can develop it on paper the better – a brief outline at least or as long a treatment as you can manage.

Screenwriter Shelley Katz fell foul of this after pitching an idea to a very well-known producer. 'He was not at all interested and asked if I had anything else. I have no idea what possessed me but stupidly I said I had this dream last night. I rarely remember my dreams but it had been a very vivid dream with a real plot line. He didn't seem at all interested. A year and a half later a film came out which was exactly my dream. I am happy to say the film tanked! Moral: always register your ideas before you pitch, even if it is just sending it to yourself registered in an unopened envelope.'

If you are worried about theft, then you can register the treatment or script with a registration agency, such as that run by the Writers Guild of America or Raindance. They will hold a copy for a given time, for a fee which can be regularly renewed. Then, if a film or programme turns up that looks suspiciously similar, it's easy to prove you wrote yours first. As Katz mentions, sometimes you can do the same by sending the script to yourself; however, this is not always as foolproof as some writers think, so make sure you get proper legal advice.

Of course, if you have used any material that comes under someone else's copyright you will need to get their permission to include it in your script, in turn.

CONFIDENTIALITY

That isn't to say that ideas go entirely unprotected. If you tell someone your idea in confidence, then you are protected under the law of confidentiality. Under this law, nobody has the right to take, repeat or use any ideas that they've been told in confidence. This would normally include pitching in a private meeting, a personal letter or email, or even a pitching competition. To be completely certain, you'd need to use the word 'confidential' in writing, either in the email or before or after a pitch meeting, but again that is rarely done except by beginners.

On the other side, production companies are becoming so concerned about being sued if they happen to produce a film that's similar to a submitted script that many are asking writers to sign a confidentiality agreement before they send anything in. This is not, I hasten to add, in an attempt to make it legal for them to steal it. The fact is some ideas are in the air and it's not uncommon for two writers or two different production companies to find themselves developing very similar stories.

Having said that, every case is different. Each country is different. Media law is complex and you should never sign anything without getting proper legal advice from an agent or an experienced media lawyer.

TO SUM UP...

- Beginners worry more about idea theft than professionals.
- There is no copyright in ideas, only how they are developed.
- Protect yourself by developing in as much detail as possible and registering the treatment or script.
- Ideas can be protected by the law of confidentiality.
- Always get proper legal advice from an agent or experienced media lawyer.

MAKING **THE APPROACH**

Once you have your polished script, it's time to approach potential buyers so that you can pitch to them for real. There are essentially four ways of making contact with the producer or agent you want to pitch to – email, social media, phone or in person. Each has its advantages and its difficulties, and you will doubtless use all of them at different times.

To add to the complications, everyone has their own preferences as to how they like to be approached – which they may or may not make public.

USING YOUR CONTACT LIST

In 'The Pitch Relationship: Them', we talked about compiling a list of possible buyers – producers, agents, production companies, development executives. Now it's time to use it to select your first contacts. As you go, you'll doubtless want to update it with new notes and added names. No matter how artistically disorganised you like to be as a writer, it's worth being organised when it comes to this list. That applies equally whether you keep your list in a sophisticated database on your computer or write it down in a book, loose-leaf binder or box file.

I believe in creating good habits. So, when I'm sending out a script, I schedule a regular time each day. That way I don't have to think or psych myself up. At that time, I simply open my producer spreadsheet and select the next name in order of priority.

Don't underestimate how long you'll need to devote to preparing each approach. For every name, you need to remind yourself who they are and why you chose them, and decide the best way to make contact. You'll probably want to visit their website for a final check and search through what they've said online, so that you can adjust what you say appropriately. You might print what you find or save it to a convenient place on the computer. (Evernote is a particularly good program for saving all kinds of research, articles, pictures, notes, etc., for easy access – and the basic version is free).

SUBMISSION GUIDELINES

Many production companies and agents give detailed guidelines for submissions on their websites. They don't do this as a joke. They've found that this is the most efficient way to deal with the mountain of applications they receive and prioritise those which are of interest to them. Take them seriously and follow their instructions precisely. To do otherwise is to declare loudly that you don't care about what they want and are not likely to be a good collaborator.

I appreciate that the guidelines may sometimes seem capricious. It can be annoying when one agent wants you to send a 500-word treatment and another insists on 150. But if they ask for 150 words, send then 150 words – or slightly under.

Don't write 'My story is so complicated that I can't do it justice in 150 words, so am sending 200.' However tough it is, find a way to do what they ask.

They will normally ask for a covering letter. Base it on your best **query letter** (see next chapter).

As I said earlier, you always want to apply to a specific person by name, but many submission guidelines ask you to send to a generic mailbox such as submissions@superagency.com. Even so, you should still address it to the producer or agent you feel would be most appropriate. You can usually add their name to your query letter in the text or subject line – such as 'For the attention of Cathy Eageragent'. The person concerned will normally be informed.

The BBC likes to direct all submissions to its Writers Room. The Writers Room is an excellent resource on one level, providing advice, hints, tips, sample scripts and all kinds of useful information. However, when it comes to submissions, it's a massive slush pile with a very low chance of your script being noticed. I'm not saying don't send it – you should send your work to anyone and everyone you feel appropriate. But once you've sent it to the Writers Room, don't hold your breath. Continue researching BBC shows for the names of producers, script editors and any other names you feel might be worth a more direct approach.

TAKING THE PLUNGE

When looking for work, inside the film industry as well as outside, most people prefer to apply to a job advert or send an email, while the least preferred method of approach is by phone or personal contact. Yet, according to statistics, personal contact and phone calls yield by far the greater success. The same applies to pitching scripts. The more personal the contact, the better.

The reason is obvious. When you apply to an advert or to a call for scripts, you are already up against thousands of other applicants. You may win, but I wouldn't bet on it. If you ring the doorbell or call by phone, it's just you. Of course, they may not want a script that day, but what have you lost?

And there's another reason. We're all human and we know instinctively how scary it is to pick up that phone or walk in that door. The fact that you had the bravery to do that speaks volumes for your commitment and desire.

When I started in the industry, I phoned all the producers whose names I spotted on the credits of programmes I liked. Often I'd get through to them. I didn't always have a script ready to pitch, so I pitched myself.

I said I was young, keen to write TV drama and wanted to learn. I offered to buy a drink if they'd share their advice – and arranged more than one valuable meeting with experienced mentors in the London Weekend bar.

This is an industry built on networking and the more people you can meet (whether you're pitching a script or yourself), the faster your career will grow.

MAKING THE CALL

Most often, the person who answers the phone will be a PA, whose job it is to protect his boss from would-be screenwriters and other nutcases. Ask for, and make a note of, their name. Today's PA may be tomorrow's senior development executive.

Remain polite. Introduce yourself. This is where you gain from having prepared and polished your personal log line (see 'What They Want').

Then explain briefly how much you admire his boss's work and how you have something you think she would be interested in. Sometimes you'll be given the brush-off – such as, 'We're fully booked up and not looking for new scripts at the moment.' It happens. They may even not be very nice about it. That happens too. Stay professional. Thank him politely and ring off – making a note in your file to try them again, maybe in six months or a year, to see if anything has changed. Then move on to the next name on your list.

Sometimes, if you make your case well, the PA might ask you to say what your project is right there and then. Don't be caught out stuttering – have your pitch ready to deliver. And listen to any comments that are made.

It's more likely that you'll be asked to send an email. Make sure you're clear on precisely what he wants you to send (what form, what information, how many words, etc.). You should have a query letter standing by for just such times. However, you will almost certainly want to glance over it, and perhaps have to change it to suit their requirements. Nonetheless, your aim should be to send it within a few minutes, or at most a few hours, of your call.

Sometimes, probably when you're least expecting it, you may find yourself put through to the producer or agent herself. She may even answer the phone in the first place.

Be prepared for all possibilities, including success.

Writer Eve Richings once called a producer's office on a Friday afternoon with an idea she wanted to pitch. 'He was the last one in and answered the phone. But he was on the point of leaving to conduct an urgent errand – buying a Lego set for his son's birthday. He said he could give me a few minutes, as long as I didn't mind meeting him outside his office and walking to a toy shop.

'Luckily I was in the area so rushed over and we walked round Hamleys together, alternately talking about Lego and my script.'

PHONING TIP – WHEN TO CALL

Many busy producers work longer hours than their assistants. To get straight through, try phoning early in the morning or after hours when he may be the only one in the office.

NO UNSOLICITED SCRIPTS

Sometimes you'll find an agent or production company will come straight out and say that they will not accept any unsolicited scripts. Read that carefully. It doesn't say they won't accept scripts, just that they must be solicited.

Don't give up, but also don't send an unsolicited script. That would be unprofessional. Your job is to get them to solicit it. How do you do that?

You make contact – by phone if possible, or by email. You tell them that you admire their work. You appreciate that they don't read unsolicited scripts and you have a script you feel would be just right for them.

Many won't, but just a few might agree to give it a look – people who wouldn't have considered your screenplay if you hadn't asked.

SOCIAL MEDIA

There is no doubt that in the future social media will play an increasing role in helping writers contact producers and agents – it's just that nobody is quite sure yet what that role will be.

On the one side, there are those – especially agents – who believe that writers should devote large amounts of time to their social media presence. One agent told me he thought all writers should be on social media no less than two hours a day.

On the other side stand those who wonder how much of all this online activity actually has any effect. And whether you wouldn't be much better off spending those two hours writing a better script.

I have spoken to writers who have made contact with agents through reading and liking each other's tweets. LinkedIn is increasingly valuable for professional interaction. One screenwriter said he'd made a valuable contact with a producer there. Facebook seems to be more useful for publicising to the public once the film or programme has been made. But the situation is constantly changing.

Increasingly, producers will check up on Google to see what you've been up to online, not least because they're thinking about how you can help publicise the finished show. Indeed, at a recent panel event, a group of BBC radio comedy producers claimed that every single comedy writer they'd picked up in the past year, they had found from the jokes they'd posted on Twitter!

The second most important advice on social media is that the emphasis is on the social. Nobody likes people who try to use the platforms solely to sell themselves. You have to be more patient and generous in your approach. Use the platforms you find most suit your style and personality. Socialise – that is to say, share useful information, interesting links, jokes, serious thoughts and ideas for the enjoyment of it. If you find a useful contact that way, so be it. But don't be pushy or self-promoting.

The most important advice, which both sides agree on, is that the script must come first. Without a good project and a good pitch, no amount of Twitter, LinkedIn or Facebook will be of any use at all.

NETWORKING EVENTS

For all the electronic media at our disposal, direct face to face contact is still the best way to build professional relationships for the future.

Most producers and agents do their best to hide away in their offices, far from anyone who might want to sell them a script, but they do understand they can't hide for ever. There are times when they come blinking into the light to meet their public – for example, at festivals, screenings and panel events.

Some events are open to any members of the public, while others are only open to members of specific groups. Search for local networking groups and organisations you can join – organisations such as Euroscript (of which I'm a director) in the UK and Shooting People.

Watch for events, too, at your local cinema, especially if it's an independent screen. You may even be able to persuade the cinema to consider inviting a given producer to a Q&A. Many industry professionals are open to being asked to talk at a screening – especially if they have a new film or programme to promote.

HOW TO MAKE AN APPROACH AT AN EVENT

After a personal appearance or panel session, the guests will usually stay around for a few minutes afterwards giving people a chance to make contact in person. Don't hang back. Popular guests will soon be surrounded and, if they're in a hurry to leave, those at the back may lose out.

Once you get to the front of the queue, there is one vital rule: *don't pitch*. They'll be too tired and distracted. They won't remember what you say and it'll make you look an amateur. Introduce yourself, be friendly and professional. You'll always get further by offering to help them, rather than starting off by asking for them to help you. For example, if there's a bar, offer to bring them a drink.

Treat the other person as a human being, with interests and needs. Your aim should always be to get them to talk more about themselves than to talk about yourself. Compliment them on something they said. This is not the time to tell them your opinion of exactly how the film industry is going wrong, and most of all not what they have done wrong themselves. Above all, be brief and to the point. Remember that they will have other people to see. Or may simply need to get home.

So, after the introductions, move on to your main goal: tell them you have a project you feel would be totally appropriate for their company and ask if they might be interested in talking further at some future date.

They will probably either say they aren't looking for anything or to contact their office.

Finally, offer your business card. (Make sure you have a good supply of professionally produced cards for any networking event. See 'Visuals and Leave-behinds'). The point of offering your card now, though, is not for them to keep it but in the hope that they will offer their own in exchange.

Shake hands and walk away. If they've given you a card, make sure you're out of sight, and then write on the back: note down where and when you met and a brief summary of what they said. This will be invaluable later – especially if you meet a number of people in quick succession, as may well happen at a good event. You'll be shocked at how quickly you'll forget who asked to see a treatment immediately and who said they weren't taking anything for six months.

You'll also need to organise all those cards you'll be collecting. They're a very valuable resource. You can scan or photograph them and paste the images into your favourite electronic contacts list. Or you can organise the cards physically, in a card index or Rolodex. One of my favourite methods is to staple the cards in alphabetical order in a spiral-bound A–Z address book. I keep it updated with notes whenever I make contact in the future, and if I go to a major festival such as Cannes I will often buy a dedicated address book solely for the piles of new cards I bring home.

Which leads me to…

FESTIVALS AND MARKETS

Film festivals and markets are excellent places to track down execs of all kinds. Each is different and has its own flavour. Some are brilliantly run with special pitching sessions and other useful events. Others are a shambles, but the warmth of the welcome makes up for the lack of organisation. In general, the most accessible festivals cater for cinema more than TV; however, that doesn't mean would-be TV writers should ignore them as cinema producers are increasingly working in TV as well.

Check out all relevant festivals, especially those close to your home town and those which seem to be right for your genre or audience. If you have a short film to offer, you may even be able to get yourself invited and paid for. Depending on where you live, you may well find there is a national agency that will help with information on the best festivals to apply to and in some cases will actively support your application. In the UK, the best people to talk to are the regional film and media agencies, as well as the British Council.

Almost all festivals offer question and answer sessions after screenings, where the director, producer or star appears in person. Many festivals also run panel discussions with a range of speakers. These sessions yield valuable information in their own right. They can help keep you up-to-date on industry attitudes, provide useful guidance on what people are looking for and new names to add to your database.

Some festivals go further and offer specific help for delegates to meet other industry professionals. They may run a market alongside, with dedicated opportunities to pitch your script, send fliers to possible buyers and seminars on industry topics. There may even be pitching competitions where you can pitch to a panel of experts in front of a live audience.

For UK and mainland European writers, I particularly recommend Rotterdam, which is a very friendly festival with a commitment to helping with project development. Berlin is a major festival and also popular with many writers. Raindance, in London, is also good –

run by and for independent filmmakers and writers, with excellent seminars and a popular Live Ammo pitching competition.

Sheffield Doc Fest is a primary festival for factual programming, offering many opportunities and competitions specifically for pitching.

In the US and Canada, AFM (American Film Market), New York and Toronto are the top festivals, but there are thousands spread across the different states during the year.

Sundance, in Park City, Utah, is one of the most highly regarded independent festivals, with a strong connection to the Sundance Institute, which offers workshops and grants throughout the year.

Check out screenwriters' festivals too. The London Screenwriters' Festival (LSF) is the largest in the world and still growing. There are sessions with a wide range of screenwriters and execs. There are fewer producers than writers, but those who attend are by definition interested in scripts. LSF also offers one-to-one pitching sessions and a script clinic, run by Euroscript. Here you can get personal feedback on your pitch, treatment or script before pitching it for real.

PITCHING AT CANNES

The leading festival and market for cinema films is Cannes – get to it if you possibly can. Producers, distributors and sales agents fly in from all over the world and there is nowhere you can learn so rapidly about the industry from the insiders who run it.

You'll need accreditation so that you can access all the industry events and go to meetings. However, depending on your status, you may find you can book a free pass. The free passes are handled by the festival (not the market which runs alongside) but nevertheless give access to all the areas you need. Check the rules and talk to others who've been accepted. The accreditation rules are complex and change almost every year. Belonging to an industry guild or union often helps and organisations such as Raindance run pre-Cannes workshops to advise writers and filmmakers who want to attend.

If all else fails, and you can raise the cash, you can buy a market pass. At the time of writing the price is between €300 and €400, depending on how far in advance you book.

You'll have to add in the costs of travel, accommodation and food (although you can often stock up calories at the many Cannes parties and lunch/evening networking events). It may sound a great deal of trouble and expense, but every day you spend in Cannes will be worth a year in terms of experience.

Cannes runs a week and a half, from Wednesday to the following Sunday – they call it Cannes Fortnight, but that's film industry accounting practice for you. However, during the first two days, producers will be far too busy trying to sell their own films to speak to anyone about new projects. So I suggest aiming to arrive in Cannes some time on the first Thursday, and staying around six nights. By the first Friday, you'll have settled in and people will be more available. Saturday and Sunday are essential, as many producers only fly in for the weekend. By Tuesday, business will be winding down, and by the second Wednesday the only people left will be those who have films in competition and are waiting for the results.

You should plan as much as you can in advance. Search your database of producers and agents and contact them to see who's going. Even if they're not, or don't want to meet, it's still worth making the call as you will thereby announce yourself as an industry person – *someone who goes to Cannes*. You should do this at least two to three weeks in advance, because as Cannes approaches, producers will be too busy preparing their own pitches.

If possible, book a meeting. You can search online for more producers who have said they are attending and add them to your list. I would also highly recommend arranging to see distributors and sales agents. You generally won't be able to sell a script to them, unless you have a package that includes a director, key cast and at least some initial finance, but they will be able to give you invaluable information about how marketable your film will be.

When you get there, you'll find many of the smaller distributors and sales agents have booths in the main market building – a concrete hulk called the Palais – while the larger companies take rooms in the main hotels. There are also offices and 'pavilions' for many film boards representing a wide range of countries, from the US and the UK to Canada and Scandinavia. These are well worth visiting as they often have information on the producers they represent. (You'll need your pass to access all these.) Most of the independent producers won't have offices at all, but you can often find them in the national pavilions. In addition, the national film boards often put on buffet or drinks parties where you can meet all kinds of producers. Ask each film board if they are having a party and try to get onto the guest list.

When arranging meetings, allow at least 30 minutes between slots – you can find yourself with a long walk to the next meeting. And you will almost always be walking. Pack a good pair of comfortable shoes, dress smart casual and expect that 90 per cent of your meetings will be postponed, cancelled or otherwise blown out. Take it in good spirit, rearrange if you can and use the spare time to network or make contact with those companies you couldn't arrange to meet before you left. Or just get talking to people you bump into – you never know who you might be standing next to in the baguette queue.

Your first task every morning is to read the free trade magazines left in all the main hotels and centres. Here you'll find information on who is attending, what they are looking for and what deals they are doing. Make notes and add any useful names to your list.

Take a large supply of business cards and leave-behinds (see 'Visuals and Leave-behinds') but don't expect to give people scripts. Producers don't want to be loaded down with excess baggage on the plane back. Have a couple of printed copies, just in case someone is desperate to read it on the spot, but mostly you'll be emailing scripts afterwards. If you're successful.

What to expect? You may not sell a script but you'll make invaluable contacts for the future. And you never know what may happen.

A few years ago, I used to advertise my Pitching Masterclass as 'What would you say to Harvey Weinstein if you met him in a lift?' One particularly committed writer used to come to all my workshops and heard me tell participants to go to Cannes and pitch. So one day he did. He organised accreditation and started working through the producers, large and small. After a time, he screwed up his courage and talked himself into the suite that had been taken by the Weinsteins, in the most expensive hotel of them all.

The writer approached the PA who was guarding the door and told her he had an appointment with Harvey.

Which he didn't.

However, as luck would have it, Harvey Weinstein was standing at that moment by one of the filing cabinets on the other side of the room. So the PA said, 'He's over there.'

He went over and Harvey happened to have a gap in his schedule so he invited him into his office and my student pitched his best idea.

'That's not one we'd take,' said Harvey. 'But I know someone who might.'

And he wrote down a name and told him where the other producer was staying. So now the student's walking down the Croisette with a note that says, 'Harvey Weinstein said you should hear this...'

What not to do in Cannes? Don't get too wound up. There'll be great highs and deep lows, successes and failures. Keep it all in perspective. Pitching at Cannes is just like pitching anywhere but more intensive.

And don't arrange to do anything at all for at least three days after you get back. You'll be too busy sleeping, filing all the business cards you've collected and sending off follow-up emails.

TO SUM UP...

- Always approach people by name.
- Check for submission guidelines.
- Phone and personal contacts are the most effective.
- You can meet producers and agents at networking events.
- Check out all your local film festivals.
- A week at the Cannes Film Festival and Market is worth years anywhere else.

THE **QUERY** LETTER

While it's always best to make contact in person, you will frequently need to pitch by email. This may be because you've not been able to speak to anyone, or because the company doesn't take phone submissions, or because the person you spoke to has asked for you to put it in writing.

What you'll use is a **query letter**. This is essentially your pitch in an email or in hard copy (sometimes known as a 'pitch on paper' or POP) and it is designed to summarise the key points of your proposal in a clear, professional way.

You should also use it as a covering letter when sending any attached material – such as an application, a synopsis, sample scenes or the whole script.

In each case, the format is simple but very precise. Producers and agents are busy people. They want to find good new writers, but they don't want to spend more time than necessary doing it. If your query letter is too long or confused, you risk them not reading it at all.

It must be short – no more than a side of A4 or letter paper – and contain the minimum information the reader needs. Four brief paragraphs of around two to three sentences each. Read that again: four paragraphs of two to three sentences. Maximum. It's not easy. But it can be done. Like your pitch, it takes clarity and ruthless editing.

The style should be brisk, pleasant and businesslike. You are selling yourself as someone who can communicate through words. So you should write in clear, direct prose.

By all means, allow the style of the email to gently echo the genre – but do it subtly. Avoid the temptation to write something silly or striking in order to stand out or you'll find yourself standing out for the wrong reason.

A comedy query letter can afford to be slightly more relaxed. A query letter for a thriller can be a little sharper. But don't fill the letter with jokes or snappy, hard-boiled aphorisms. Leave that to the script.

SUBJECT LINE

The subject line should clearly state what the email is about, including the script title if appropriate. Such as:

Feature screenplay proposal: Sunset over Sarajevo

Or:

Representation for cinema and TV screenwriter Angela Keenscribe

Your subject line should never be vague or generic such as 'Enquiry' or 'Great idea' – or attempt forced bonhomie, such as 'Have I got a script for you!' or 'Do you want to be scared?' And it should certainly not be blank.

Emails with such subjects will make you look like an amateur or a spammer – and probably be trashed unread.

LAYOUT

Unlike scripts, there is no prescribed font for a query letter. Use one of the standard readable fonts, say Times New Roman or Arial. This is not the time for Comic Sans or Shiver, no matter how appropriate they may seem to your genre. And don't use Courier. Keep that for the script itself.

If you are sending the query letter as an attachment, lay the paragraphs out neatly, with generous margins and white space between them. And paste the text into the body of your email as well

– why make them go to the effort of opening the attachment (and risk that they don't. Or for some technical reason can't).

DEAR (NAME)

In the 'To' window, you put the name of your selected target. If submission guidelines insist on a generic mailbox, then add 'For the attention of' or 'FAO' followed by the name.

In the body of the letter and email, put 'Dear (first name)'. Although 'Hi' is common, I'd still err on the side of formality until you know them better. However, Mr or Mrs (surname) is too formal. If you feel very awkward addressing a very high-level producer by his first name, then use both first name and surname (as in 'Dear Harvey Weinstein'…).

And *get their name right!* Watch out in particular for names that have similar spellings (Alastair and Alistair, Claire and Clare) and names that get easily confused. People generally like their names, and usually prefer them as they are. For some reason, Charles is often confused with Chris or even, bizarrely, Richard. When someone emails me as Chris or Richard I don't ignore the email but I make a mental note that this person is either very busy or very sloppy. Actually, strike that: the busy people invariably take the trouble to get it right.

So go online, Google their name and make absolutely sure you have every letter in the right place.

PARAGRAPH ONE – WHY YOU'RE WRITING

In the first paragraph you lay out the reason why they should read on. Don't start with a preamble or clever introduction. Nor is this the place to show your brilliant wit or skin-crawling ability to strike fear into readers' hearts. If a busy executive can't tell why you're writing to them in the first two lines he'll probably bin the letter there and then. Make it quick and simple.

Something like:

I am seeking representation for myself as a screenwriter for cinema and TV. I have just completed a new rom-com screenplay, JOBS FOR GIRLS, and notice that you represent Beatrice Burnheart, whose writing I love.

I am looking for a producer for my conspiracy screenplay SUNSET OVER SARAJEVO. I saw and very much liked your recent thriller Roses for Winter *and feel that my script would fit right in with your company's style.*

I'm sure you will have much more to say, but at this point your priority is to say why you are contacting them, and for them to understand why they should continue reading.

With that first short paragraph under your belt you move on to...

PARAGRAPH TWO – THE PITCH

Here's where you bring out your finely honed pitch. You may want to make slight adjustments to suit who you're writing to. Obviously, if you've already mentioned something, such as the genre, in your previous paragraph, you don't repeat it here. Otherwise, you simply insert your best, crispest, most powerful log line.

JOBS FOR GIRLS is an offbeat comedy about a straight-laced junior manager in a large company who finds herself alone in a sit-in with a madcap anarchist who doesn't believe in playing by the rules.

A maverick ecologist discovers an international energy corporation has been hiding unstable nuclear waste under the world's poorer cities and killed the last expert who threatened to expose them. To save his life, and the lives of millions, he must learn to trust and work with others.

That's it. The pitch and nothing but the pitch.

PARAGRAPH THREE - YOU

In the third paragraph, you lay out why you are absolutely the best person to have written this script. Once more, you only have two to three sentences, so choose your strongest personal log line and the most powerful and relevant item on your CV.

It goes without saying that, quite aside from writing the best script you possibly can, you need to have done some planning about what you can put in this paragraph. If you have any personal connection with the story, put it here. Maybe you have a background in the subject. Even if it's only the research you did to write the script. If you have nothing else, then talk about the contacts you've made.

This is where you draw on the social media and blogging work I suggested you do in 'What They Want'. Here, also, give the best of any relevant credits you've gained, prizes won, competition shortlist places. Many producers will scan the first line of a query letter and then jump to the third paragraph before they even read the pitch. What they are looking for is some kind of independent validation. Ideally, something that involves money or some other significant support or credibility.

WHAT *NOT* TO PUT IN THERE?

That you showed it to another producer and he thought it was great. (If he thought it was so great, why didn't he buy it?) Testimonials from people in the industry are meaningless, unless they actually paid you something or otherwise got involved.

Don't put that you went on screenwriting courses (wonderful as many are), gained a screenwriting MA (unless your story revolves around people taking a screenwriting MA), that the screenplay was liked by your mum, friend, a friend of a friend who once knew someone who worked at the BBC.

Don't write that you've had great feedback from a professional reader. Great that you've sent it to a reader, but not relevant here.

I once received a query letter from a writer (who shall remain nameless) who used this paragraph to quote detailed feedback he'd received. To make things worse, not only was some of the assessment highly critical, but he went on to say that he hadn't actually done anything about it yet. I still can't work out what he thought telling me this would achieve.

Finally, don't put that you have future collaborators attached unless they are the kind of star names who would actually 'open' the movie – i.e. attract an audience. There are a few A-list actors and directors whose names will add to the box-office take or TV ratings, but very, very few. Don't tell the reader you have interest from an actor who once had a walk-on part in *EastEnders*. Or any crew members – no matter how prestigious. Sadly, no one queues round the block or turns on a TV series because of the director of photography.

If you do have interest from someone big, then you must get them to sign a letter of intent. This has absolutely no legal power but it is enormously difficult to obtain nonetheless. So if you have a letter of intent from a top director or actor, that's definitely worth bragging about.

Here are a few samples for the third paragraph:

I run a highly popular comic blog on jobs for women, Gurlijobs, which has over a thousand followers. I have also had five short films produced and my comedy-drama treatment 'Needle and Fred' was nominated for an award in this year's Heartsleeve Screenwriting Competition.

I myself worked as an ecologist in the former Yugoslavia and have seen from the inside the tricks that the major energy companies get up to. I have had articles commissioned by local newspapers and national ecology magazines.

So now that you've convinced the reader you are worth reading, you…

PARAGRAPH FOUR – SIGN OFF

All the paragraphs are short. The last is the shortest. You've done the job. Finish as briefly as you can. Tell the reader the current state of the project, how you might proceed or what you're attaching:

I look forward greatly to the possibility of meeting you and discussing this further.

I have a completed, polished screenplay running 98 pages and would be pleased to send it to you.

I attach the synopsis and short proposal you ask for, as per your submission guidelines.

This is followed by *Yours sincerely* or *Kind regards*, your name and your contact details.

For a documentary query letter you'll also want to include a link to your online trailer (see 'Visuals and Leave-behinds').

CHECK AND CHECK AGAIN

Before you send it – check the letter through and then check it again. Check it for mistakes, missing words, typos and spelling. Check the recipient's name one more time.

For some reason, we always make mistakes with the most important words. If you are an expert on Formula One racing, then those are the words I guarantee you're most likely to mistype. Perhaps we tend to skim over what we know well and concentrate most on what we find difficult. In any case, check, check, check.

If your email system allows it, I recommend setting it so that it queues emails before sending. I've lost count of the number of times I had a new thought just a few minutes after finishing a query letter. If it's already been sent, it's too late. Queue the email, give yourself five or ten minutes in case of second thoughts, and then press send.

It's done. Move on.

57 Shakespeare Towers
Grub Street
Wolverston WX7 3YK

Tel: 03069 990817
Mob: 07700 900342
Email: akeenscribe@jawsinspace.com

Attn. Felicity Moneymaker
Moneymaker and Quill Literary Agency
101 Fame Street
Barchester BC9 1AZ

Dear Felicity Moneymaker

Representation for cinema and TV screenwriter Angela Keenscribe – *Jobs for Girls*

I am seeking representation for myself as a screenwriter for cinema and TV. I have just completed a new rom-com screenplay, JOBS FOR GIRLS, and notice that you represent Beatrice Burnheart, whose writing I love.

JOBS FOR GIRLS is an offbeat comedy about a straight-laced junior manager in a large company who finds herself alone in a sit-in with a madcap anarchist who doesn't believe in playing by the rules.

I run a highly popular comic blog on women's employment, Gurljobs, which has over a thousand followers. I have also had five short films produced and my comedy-drama treatment 'Needle and Fred' was nominated for an award in this year's Heartsleeve Screenwriting Competition.

I attach the synopsis and short proposal you ask for as per your submission guidelines.

Yours sincerely

Angela Keenscribe

Angela Keenscribe

SAMPLE QUERY LETTER

TO SUM UP...

- A query letter must be short – no longer than a single sheet or equivalent.
- Always try to send it to a named person – and get the name right!
- The subject and first paragraph should clearly introduce why you're writing.
- The second paragraph is your pitch on paper.
- The third shows why you are the right person to have written the script.
- Put your contact details at the end.
- Double and triple check before sending.

THE PITCH **MEETING**

Then it happens. After the hundredth attempt (or maybe the very first) you land a meeting. You receive a positive reply to an email, someone invites you over the phone or you walk into an office at a festival or market. It's real. You're going to be face to face.

Don't go in unprepared.

PREPARING FOR THE MEETING

Do your homework. Get back onto the internet and add to the research you've already done on this producer, agent or company. See if there are any interviews she's given on YouTube or elsewhere. Prepare yourself for possible questions.

Decide what to wear. Smart casual is the rule. You don't want to turn up in a suit but you also shouldn't wander in wearing shorts and a ripped T-shirt. I knew a writer who used to pitch in a colourful, floral, short-sleeved shirt, feeling that this made him memorable. It did, but he was known for wearing a colourful shirt, rather than for his ideas.

If you have a signature dress style, make sure it doesn't outshine your work.

Find a quiet place where you can rehearse your pitch out loud. Some people like to record their voice or take a video. Everything helps.

You should certainly practise pitching to as many other people as you can before you pitch it to someone whose reaction counts. This is scary. Get over it. It's fine to be scared. It's not fine to be unprepared. (There's more on how to prepare psychologically and build your confidence in 'Pitching to a Room'.)

However, you don't have to be word perfect. This is a conversation. Nor do you have to have a great speaking voice or be brilliantly funny. They're looking for a writer not a performer.

Talking of which, there is a story that two writers once hired Kevin Spacey to come to a pitch meeting with them and perform their pitch. I'm sure he was very good. Having said that, walking into the room with Kevin Spacey would probably have clinched the deal before he opened his mouth.

GOING TO THE MEETING

It shouldn't need saying, but be on time. Actually, aim to be well ahead of time. It's better to sit in a coffee bar nearby for an hour than to run in five minutes late. If you're not familiar with the area, allow longer for finding your way. These are busy people and being late for any reason short of a national emergency is the height of disrespect.

And yes, they may well keep you sitting in reception until long after the appointed time. That's how it goes. In the future, when you've won a handful of Oscars and can command millions for a single script, you can do the same if you wish. Although in my experience, the writers, producers and agents who are really at the top are usually the nicest and the least likely to need to prove how important they are.

If your meeting is postponed or cancelled at the last minute, take it with good grace. It happens. A film suddenly needs urgent attention. A client goes into meltdown. The producer has to fly abroad at a few hours' notice. Or a vital meeting has simply overrun.

Be polite and professional and suggest some possible times to reschedule.

On my first visit to Cannes, my producer David Castro and I walked into the hotel suite of a major independent Hollywood producer. This man was currently on a roll, having produced a major hit, and we didn't think he'd bother to give us the time of day, but to our surprise his assistant booked us in for eight o'clock the next morning. The next day we turned up early and he didn't arrive. We waited half an hour. Still nothing.

We'd obviously been blown out – it was clear to us that the big name producer had never meant to see us at all. We had made an effort to get up especially early and could have made a fuss, but instead we politely left our mobile numbers and went looking for breakfast. Fifteen minutes later, as we contemplated whether we could afford the hotel's five-star rates for a cup of coffee, my phone rang. Were we still nearby? The producer had in fact been dealing with an unexpected crisis but now he was back.

In the event, he bought us breakfast, didn't buy the script, but became a good contact – one whom I always met up with in Cannes in the following years.

Even as you wait for the pitch meeting to take place, you can make active use of your time. Look at the posters on the wall of reception – what do they tell you about the company? Do they display their biggest hits (useful to know what productions they are most proud of)? Many companies will leave out brochures and other printed material. Take them, read them and keep them for your files. Others will provide copies of the latest trades for visitors to read.

Agents will almost certainly display work by their clients – advertising posters and books. Study them carefully – they are telling you whom they represent and what genres they prefer.

Remember, as you wait you are on view. Be professional. This is not the time to have an argument over the phone. Tempting as it may be, this is also not the time to listen to your iPod or catch up on writing your next script. It can look awkward if the producer appears and you have to take up time stuffing things away in your bag. And if you really must use your mobile to play Battleships, make sure it's on silent and nobody can see the screen.

IN THE MEETING

The producer comes out and you shake hands. You follow her into her office. What happens now?

What *doesn't* happen is that you pitch. These first minutes are crucial in establishing rapport. Don't blow all the good work you've done so far by treating the other person in the room as a target. Treat her as a human being.

Producer Anita Lewton advises, 'Smile, relax and introduce yourself and anyone who's come to the meeting with you. It really helps people remember you and puts them at ease.'

What you are doing here is setting up a relationship that may last for a few minutes – or for many years. Whether you sell this one script is less important than whether you begin building a connection for the future.

I like to start by asking a few questions, just as I would when meeting someone in everyday life. I ask the producer how she is, how her work is going, whether she's having a good day. If in a festival, I ask how the festival has been for her so far.

You're establishing yourself as someone who isn't just another wannabe, but a fellow professional. Albeit one who is lower down the ladder. Someone they can imagine working with. Producers are so used to being pitched to, it often takes them momentarily by surprise that the other person even cares enough to ask.

When my fellow producers and I first went to Cannes with our plans for the movie *Paradise Grove*, we'd make a point of not pitching as we sat down but engaging co-producers in conversation.

I remember taking an impromptu meeting with a busy British producer and sales agent. We hadn't been able to book a meeting in advance, but it so happened he had five minutes free. He sat at the end of a long table, head down, clearly very tired, patiently waiting for us to pitch.

We didn't. David asked how his Cannes had been so far. The man looked up at us in surprise and for the first time actually took proper notice of us, before sharing some of the problems he was having right then.

127

He became a good friend and useful source of advice for years afterwards. Your ability to ask questions and listen are perhaps your most valuable assets – more valuable than your ability to open your mouth.

ANYTHING BUT VAMPIRES!

One of the most off-putting things that can happen in the initial conversation is that you learn your producer has stopped making the genre you came to pitch. There's not a lot you can do about this, except to accept it.

Say something like, 'What a shame. I saw all those films on your backlist and that's precisely the kind of project I've come to pitch. Would you prefer it if I talked to you about something else instead?'

She may be interested in hearing your pitch anyway, or she may ask if you have anything in a different genre. (You will, won't you? See Response 3 in the next chapter.)

Naz Sadoughi was told the following story by a screenwriter friend who was called into a meeting by a Hollywood studio:

'He's prepared a couple of pitches, one for a dystopian vampire movie and another about artificial intelligence (which were in vogue). However, before he sits down one of the execs jokes that they can't wait to hear his pitch as long as it doesn't involve vampires or robots!

'Breaking out in a cold sweat, feeling dizzy and thinking he's well and truly screwed, he takes his seat. All eyes are on him as he fidgets not knowing what to do – he has to make something up – but his mind's gone blank! So he starts to recount how, earlier that day, while helping a friend move house, he'd had the misfortune of dealing with the worst removal man in the whole of the city. He explains step by step the catalogue of disasters and mishaps so that by the end the panel are crying with laughter.

'Thinking he now has to confess to his vampire and A.I. story ideas, he notices the producers are already up on their feet shaking his hand. They're telling him what a great idea he has and how they can't wait to read the new script about the worst removals man in LA...'

THE PITCH

After a certain length of time, the other person will ask, 'So what have you got for me?'

At last – this is your chance to pitch. At this point, you'll probably feel a desperate urge to apologise: you're not really ready, you're very young, very old, very stressed out... Never say you're sorry before you pitch. Or indeed afterwards. You are there, you have been asked to say what you have.

What if you weren't expecting to pitch? Sometimes people invite you for a generalised 'meet and greet'. The idea behind a meet and greet is exactly as it sounds. You make contact and have a conversation. And there is no expectation that you will pitch a specific idea.

Even then, you should always be ready. You never know when someone is about to ask: 'What have you got?'

And when they do...

You pause, breathe, smile pleasantly, look them in the eye and deliver your one-to-two-sentence log line pitch.

You do this confidently, because you've already used the pitch many times and you know it works. You also know that the script works.

What you *never* do with the pitch, under any circumstances, is read it. Nothing is more valuable to you at this stage than eye contact. Remember, this is a conversation. What you are doing is rehearsing what those two friends will say to each other at the bus stop or water fountain.

If you can't manage two sentences about the script you have slaved over for months, possibly years, then who can? This is your baby.

If you are worried that you may hesitate, stumble or generally get something wrong, then yes, that's possible. But it doesn't matter. In normal life, people make mistakes, correct themselves and pause for thought. In fact, a perfect reading can sound rather cold and off-putting. Whereas taking your time and pausing for thought can feel warm and engaging. It draws people in.

I have run my pitching workshops for many years now and every time, despite having been told it doesn't work, someone inevitably tries to read their pitch to the group. I let them finish and then confiscate their notes and tell them to say the pitch again. Every time, they are convinced they won't remember what to say. But they invariably do. More importantly, I then ask the rest of the writers for their feedback and they always find the second version was infinitely more persuasive than when it was read. Eye contact is key.

So, to repeat, *you look the producer in the eye, trust yourself and you say your log line pitch.*

AND THEN YOU STOP.

This is perhaps the most difficult part of all. You are filled with ideas and desperate to impress. You know how much you left out and how many questions the producer must have. You are also only too aware of the fluffs you made, all the mistakes – how it was nothing like as good as it was in the bathroom mirror this morning.

But you don't say any of that.

You don't continue gabbling in the hope of filling in all the stuff you want her to understand.

You leave a silence.

Remember, your goal is for her to say 'Send me the script' or 'Tell me more'. How can she do that if you're still talking? I've seen writers talk themselves out of a potential deal merely by saying too much.

I once helped organise a five week speed-dating workshop between writers from the Screenwriters' Workshop and producers from the New Producers' Alliance. On the last evening, the ten writer-producer pairs were given eight minutes each to pitch their film to us – a panel of writers and producers – to win a year's development support.

We made a point of asking them to be brief so we had time to ask questions. Despite this, all but two of the ten pairs were still talking at the eight-minute mark without having paused once to let us speak, comment, praise or give feedback!

Silence is frightening – and most people will do anything to fill it with talk. Which is why it's so important for you to stop after your log line pitch. Let the listener feel the pressure to say something. And she will.

TO SUM UP...

- Do your homework.
- Get to the meeting early.
- Spend the first minutes asking questions and listening.
- Never read your pitch.
- Say your log line and then stop.

THE RESPONSE

You've met, you've talked, you've pitched, you've stopped so that she can speak. What happens next depends entirely on what she says.

RESPONSE 1 – THIS IS NOT FOR ME

This is a very possible reply and the first thing to realise is that it may carry absolutely no criticism of your pitch. However excellent your idea, it may be the wrong genre for her, or the wrong timing.

Being rejected is painful but it's nothing to be ashamed of. The trick is dealing with it and keeping on.

At the start of his career screenwriter Paul Mendelson pitched a film idea to the celebrated feature director Nic Roeg:

'It was a story about a Jewish ghost. Roeg read it, but did nothing with it. A year later, he found himself working in the next-door office to Verity Lambert, the TV producer, and suggested she read it. She liked it, contacted me and advised me to turn it into a half hour, which I did, and then sent it to the Head of Comedy at the BBC.

'He liked the script but proceeded to tell me all the things he objected to – suspension of disbelief, ethnic humour, special effects, dogs....

'So now I knew what to do next – a sitcom with no Jews or dogs. I went away and wrote a script about a (non-Jewish) lawyer who falls in love with a woman half his age – *May to December*. The BBC loved it and asked for a second episode, to prove the first wasn't a fluke. It wasn't and the show ran for six series.

'By now everything had changed. *Ghost* had been a major hit in the cinema and so ghosts were in. Maureen Lipman had just starred in a series of popular British Telecom commercials as Beattie, a funny Jewish mother. So Jewish mothers were in. I sent *So Haunt Me* again and it was as if he hadn't seen it before. It played to audiences of around 13 million per show and went on to run for three seasons plus a one-hour special.

'It's all about timing. Everything I've done has been rejected some time.'

RESPONSE 2 – THIS IS NOT FOR ME AND THIS IS WHY

You'll probably never find out why your pitch has been rejected. You can try asking politely what didn't work for her, but she's not your teacher and she may not feel inclined to say much more. She may not even know why she didn't respond well. Most producers and agents react on instinct and aren't necessarily adept at putting their reasons into words. It's not always easy to work out precisely why a pitch didn't strike sparks.

Nevertheless, if you are lucky enough to be given feedback, listen carefully. If she launches into detail, you might ask if you can take notes. In fact, it's a sign of respect to take notes. Sometimes, I give detailed feedback to a writer who sits and nods but doesn't write down a word. I wonder to myself if they have the powers of Mr Memory or simply have no intention of taking notice of what I say! It doesn't feel very respectful.

Of course, the feedback you get may be right or it may be wrong. Some people say you should ignore any feedback from someone who's rejected your pitch – even the compliments. There may be reasons for the rejection that the producer can't or won't tell you – so she may invent something.

It's also true that some feedback can be weird – or just plain wrong. It may be that it simply isn't the kind of story they like. If someone who prefers comedy criticises your horror pitch for not being funny enough, then you can probably safely ignore it. People have odd prejudices. I once met a distributor who told me she never bought a documentary if it had a snake in it.

Mendelson tells how his third series was originally pitched as *Home Is the Hero*: 'This was the story of an alien superhero who tries to pass as human but can't understand human customs. I pitched it to the latest Head of Comedy who said, "I like everything about it except the superhero bit!"'Mendelson changed the title to *My Hero*, waited a year and submitted it to a different producer as 'people don't like to commission something that's been in before'. The new producer loved the idea and *My Hero* ultimately ran for six series.

Some people will be entirely negative. You start to wonder whether you can salvage anything at all from the wreckage. It may sound strange, but you should take strong criticism as a compliment. Nobody wastes time criticising someone who has no future. Their intensity, albeit painful, is a sign that they feel you have potential.

However, most producers will do their best to find something positive to say. Listen to what they praise. It's too easy to hear only the criticisms and forget to hear what they liked. But this is also useful feedback, telling you which parts of the pitch to build on for next time.

If three or more people all come out with variations of the same criticism, then you should take it seriously. It may be that they are right, it may be that they are wrong, but somehow you are leading them to expect something different. For example, you said something that made them expect a comedy when it isn't.

HOW TO LISTEN TO CRITICISM AND TAKE SUGGESTIONS

It's much easier to say when a pitch is going wrong than to know how to put it right. What you absolutely must not do is argue back. It doesn't matter how much she's misunderstood or how awful her ideas sound at first. It's possible that there's something in the wording of the pitch that caused the misunderstanding. Listen to what she's saying, and you may realise how the misunderstanding arose, and how you can avoid it in future.

In any case, trying to convince a producer that she's wrong and you are right is a losers' game. Remember, it's not just about one pitch; it's about a career. Think in the long term. This person who is rejecting your idea today could be a valuable collaborator tomorrow. Fighting her only makes her less likely to want to listen to you in the future. Furthermore, you have no reason to argue. Until you sign a contract, you're in charge of your script. Up till then, you don't have to do what anyone says. You can write and pitch whatever you want.

However, two heads are often better than one, and an outsider may come up with a useful idea that it would be foolish to throw away. If her suggestions are good ones, you'd be an idiot not to use them. You don't have to pay her and you'll get all the credit.

Feedback can come in different forms. First is the critical comment that is absolutely right on the mark. You generally know if that's the case, because it really hurts! The temptation is to reject it heatedly. After a while, you realise that the heat comes from the very fact that the producer has hit a nerve. It may take a few minutes, hours or even days, but slowly it sinks in that she's right and you'd better do something about it.

Second is the feedback that is so widely off target that it's almost laughable. As with the woman who told me she never bought documentaries that showed snakes. These should be rightly dismissed. (Unless, of course, you find everyone telling you the same apparently laughable thing. When Paul Mendelson pitched *So Haunt Me* it was probably true that audiences didn't respond well to Jewish mothers and ghosts. When the audience response changed, the project became doable.)

Third, there's the criticism which requires you to read between the lines. This is trickier. Even producers who are highly experienced at giving feedback don't always know exactly what they are reacting to. For example, three different people may criticise three different parts of your log line. One might quibble over the genre. Another over the protagonist's goal. A third with the way you end it.

The real problem may lie, say, with the inner flaw, which nobody mentioned, but which is the real reason why the genre, goal and ending of the pitch all misfire. So you need to stand back and take a view. If a number of people find problems, then accept that a problem exists, though you don't always have to agree with the diagnosis.

Finally, many suggestions can be taken in two ways. Let's say a producer likes your idea, but thinks it's too dark. Obviously one response would be to lighten it. This may work well for you, or it may turn your story into something so different that it's no longer the story you wanted to tell. The counterintuitive move, then, might be to do the reverse and actually make the story darker.

This often works because many pitches fail by being neither one thing nor the other. Tim Bevan, co-chairman of Working Title, who has been behind more successful films than most producers in the world, says the biggest problem he sees is mediocrity.

If your pitch is stuck in the mediocre middle, then shifting in either direction will be better than staying where you are.

If you establish a reputation for being a good professional, good at listening and considering other people's ideas, your pitch meeting will have been worthwhile – sale or no sale.

RESPONSE 3 –
THIS IS NOT FOR ME BUT WHAT ELSE DO YOU HAVE?

This is a great response. Yes, she turned it down, but you've shown you're good enough for her to consider working with you – that you might have other interesting ideas to discuss. Have you?

Try to go into any pitch meeting with at least three or four log lines that you can bring out in case you're asked. Preferably in different genres. If possible, for scripts you've already written! If you have no other current ideas, then spend a little time in advance developing some.

If you find in your initial conversation that none of them will fit what she wants, your only option is to improvise. Make up a few embryo ideas. One thing that divides the amateur writer from the professional is that professionals become adept at coming up with ideas on the spot.

In the heat of the moment, you may even find yourself creating a really good concept. In which case, the moment you get out of the room write it down.

Shelley Katz tells a story about a screenwriter who, lost for ideas, improvised a dazzling pitch on the spot. 'The producer loved it and the writer went home to work it up into a treatment only to find that next day he couldn't remember a word of what he'd said.'

The moral of the story – don't rely on your memory – as soon as possible make detailed notes of everything that was discussed.

TO SUM UP...

- **Being rejected comes with the job – it's nothing to be ashamed of. Sometimes it's simply a matter of timing.**
- **Listen to all feedback.**
- **You don't need to argue – take what you need.**
- **Feedback comes in different forms and sometimes you need to read between the lines.**

THE RESPONSE (CONTINUED)

And then, increasingly, if you do your work and keep improving your pitches, the responses will become more positive.

RESPONSE 4 - TELL ME MORE

Well done. You've said enough to pique her interest, and now she has questions. This doesn't mean your pitch should have been longer – it means it did its job.

What you do not do now, though, is launch into telling the whole story. Don't allow yourself to get trapped into a dread recitation of *'...and then... and then...'*

In fact, I'd avoid telling her the story altogether. If she wants the full story, she'll normally ask to see the script – or possibly a short treatment/synopsis (see 'Visuals and Leave-behinds').

What she wants from you now is the highlights – a verbal trailer, a glimpse of character, an exciting moment or two.

EXAMPLE

Take the conspiracy thriller I sketched out in the Query Letter. If I were creating a verbal trailer for the movie, I'd paint out a dramatic scene with the ecologist – plunging him into a conflict that shows his strengths and flaws. I'd then jump to a key turning point and show the challenge he now faces and the decision he makes. I might end with a scene that evoked a gripping sense of fear.

Essentially, in doing this I'm creating a log line for each scene – two to three sentences each – using the most evocative language I can to bring them to life. In building your verbal trailer it's important to draw on strong, active language that draws on the senses. Tell us what we would see, but also what we hear and what we feel as the action unfolds.

....

EXERCISE – **CREATING A VERBAL TRAILER**

Create a verbal trailer for your script. Keep it short. No more than three key scenes, each of which shows a different angle on the script: one that shows an intriguing side of your main character or characters; one that brings to life a crucial plot twist; and one that builds the emotion of the genre.

Watch film and TV trailers in your genre. In the cinema, on TV and on the internet. Look at the kinds of scenes they select. Why did they choose them? What is the point that's being made? Obviously visual trailers are longer and more complex than you'd want for a verbal trailer in a pitch meeting. Which three scenes would you select for a verbal trailer if you needed to make one?

....

LANGUAGE

In daily life, we use language which reflects our five senses – sight, sound, feeling, smell and taste. We not only sense the world through them, but also use them to think and communicate. So we have the strongest impact when we use phrases that draw on our senses – That *looks* as if it will work – I like the *sound* of that – It gives me a warm *feeling* – etc.

By contrast, abstract language (*he realises, she thinks, we understand*) evokes no sensory impressions at all and so lacks that essential vitality. It has its uses, but tends to make a presentation sound rather thin and passionless.

Drawing widely on the different kinds of sensory language will bring your pitch to life.

....

EXERCISE - **ADDING EVOCATIVE LANGUAGE TO YOUR TRAILER**

Go back to the verbal trailer you created just now and note the kind of language you're using. Are you employing abstract/ academic words and phrases or evoking sensory impressions? Or a mixture of the two? See (hear and feel) where you can give your descriptions more energy by adding sensory language.

Sight – Film is a visual medium so you should be making sure that your listeners see pictures in their minds. Include vivid visuals and visual descriptions (the explosion *lights up* the sky) and also metaphor (he *sees* what she's been saying to him all along).

Hearing – Refer to what we would hear in a scene (a door *creaks* in the darkness...) and use metaphors (they work *in harmony* together... the plan *sounds* dangerous...).

Feeling – Both emotional and physical feelings (she is *desperate* to survive... he *feels* the treacherous ice under his feet...) and again metaphorical (she *grasps* the opportunity... he *forces* his way to the top of the company...).

Although less prominent than the first three don't neglect the power of the sense of *smell* (the plan *stinks*...).

And *taste* (a *sweet* moment...).

Using strong, evocative sense impressions will draw a producer in and ensure she engages her cinematic imagination in full.

....

TELLING THE STORY

If the producer specifically asks you to tell her the story, you must still not launch into a lengthy outline. Adopt a similar approach as for your verbal trailer. Give her four key turning points – what kicks the story off, the first big decision that your protagonist makes, how it all goes wrong and the final battle. Make your description brief and dramatic, using vivid sensory language as above to bring the scenes to life. And with each scene, sketch in how it challenges your main character, forcing him to face the possibility of change. No more than six to ten sentences at most.

If she asks you to give her the ending – you absolutely must do so. Many writers protest at this. Won't you ruin the suspense? What if there's a big twist at the finish – won't you blow the surprise? Don't you want her to find out by reading the script?

Yes, to all these. But if she's asked you for the end, you must tell her. Your story's ending, as we've seen, provides meaning to the whole. If she doesn't know how it finishes, she can't properly judge where you're going with the script. The ending may not work. You may not even know how to end it. She doesn't want to waste her time reading your screenplay only to find it falls apart in the last act.

As for spoiling the suspense, you have to trust that she's a professional. She understands that the audience will be intrigued, surprised, shocked as the story progresses and she will take that into account if and when she finally reads the script. Don't be coy; deliver.

Here are some other questions that you need to have answers to. Prepare for them – and as many others as you can think of. And understand that there will always be questions you couldn't have thought of in advance – so be ready to tap dance on the spot.

AUDIENCE

What is the core audience/market?

You don't need to speak in social demographics (and indeed shouldn't). On the other hand, you shouldn't be too vague or all-inclusive. The programme that's aimed at everyone is aimed at no one. In any case, nobody will believe you if you say the audience is everyone. Or even everyone between the ages of 14 and 24.

Describe your ideal viewers. What do they love? Do they read newspapers or spend their life on Snapchat? What films, programmes, activities do they like? Are they teenagers who watched every episode of *True Blood*? Or are they older, politically aware, readers of serious magazines who are passionate about injustice?

Ask yourself, who would love this story – who would want to be or to follow your protagonist – who would want to spend time in the world you depict?

DIFFERENCE

What makes your project special? What makes it stand out?

If you've found the right people to pitch to, they will be expert in your genre. You need to know as much about it, if not more. Be aware of all the rival shows that are like yours. Do your research. One advantage of practising your pitch widely is that many people will spontaneously suggest parallels with other films and programmes they've seen. Check them out. Find out why yours is different from the others and be prepared to say so.

If a producer mentions a possible competitor, you should be ready to explain what makes yours stand out. If it is, by bad luck, one you've never heard of, ask her about it – her description may well provide the answer you need. Otherwise, thank her for the suggestion and say you'll check it out immediately.

TRANSMEDIA

Do you see any opportunity for spin-offs? Cross-platform opportunities?

Producers are always looking for ways to cover the financial risks. Anything that raises extra avenues for publicity – or indeed income – is to be welcomed. In the past, this would have focused on merchandising. Nowadays, you can add a whole range of new media. You don't need to be a transmedia expert, but you should spend a little time thinking about how your story could be publicised or exploited in different forms.

Is there potential for a blog with character bios and even games for fans to play? An app? How could social media be used to develop the audience? A Twitter account for your central character? A Facebook page? A spoof website for the overpaid football team that your protagonist is trying to beat?

Can you see possibilities for a web series? In creating new subplots for spin-offs? Background stories of the characters? Bonus storylines? Is there room to build up the world of the story? Have you cut characters and scenes from earlier drafts that could work here?

What is your distribution strategy?

Some factual programmes – such as educational and social impact documentaries – aim to change the world. With such genres, your distribution strategy becomes an important part of the pitch.

How would you ensure your film engages with the world it intends to affect? You should develop ideas of how you are going to add to the impact of the programme – running workshops, interactive websites, games, social media immersion, etc.

CHARACTERS

Tell me about the main character.

The playwright Ibsen used to say that in the first draft your characters are distant acquaintances and as you work they become friends and then family. Know your characters intimately and be prepared to talk about them – especially your protagonist and antagonist. What makes them tick? What work do they do? What is their passion? What do they hate? What is their life goal? What is their goal in the story? What is their journey – how do they change by the end? Or fail to change?

Tell me about the characters.

You may be asked about the characters in general. This is a big subject and the danger is that you will begin to ramble. Once more, the aim is to keep it energetic and short. Focus on three or four key roles and link them to their place in the story, for example:

- Main character – her personality, her flaws, her strengths, her life at the start, her work, her goals in life and in the script, her journey.

- Second character – how he helps her by doing X, his flaws, his strengths, his change (if any).

- Antagonist – how she blocks the main character by doing Y, her flaws, her strengths, her passions and hatreds.

- Fourth character – how he surprises us by turning out to be Z, his initial appearance, how he reveals his true self.

Who do you see in the cast?

Prepare an ideal wish-list for the main roles. It's great if you can come up with some realistic names. It shows you're thinking professionally and helps create pictures of the characters in your listener's head. You should try to be aware of the current trends and which actors are popular in which fields. However, be sensible. Don't start suggesting Brad Pitt or Meryl Streep for your no-budget indie horror movie.

Having said that, there are some well-known actors who are known for their willingness to take parts in small but interesting cinema or TV, especially if the right director is on board. So, again, do your research. There's no harm in saying, 'I know it's a long shot but there's a cameo that I'd love to see played by...'

COLLABORATION AND FLEXIBILITY

Are you open to change?

This is a delicate one. You need to show confidence in your idea – so you shouldn't volunteer to start changing things before you're asked – otherwise you begin to sound unsure about your own pitch.

However, a producer or agent may well test you out, to see what kind of collaborator you would be. Or she may see an opportunity to improve the saleability of your project by making alterations. She may suggest changes to a main character – adjusting their gender, age, race or job. She may want to consider altering the world of the story – trying out a new venue or social setting, or shifting into the past – or future.

If she does, the trick is to sound open-minded. Remember, you don't have to argue the point now. They haven't even read the script yet. There's no reason to go into battle over whether your protagonist is a man or a woman, or 17 years old or 70. It is quite possible that they might come up with an idea that will lift your script to a higher level. And there's an equal chance that they'll come up with something seriously bad.

Whatever they suggest, you should sound enthusiastically interested in their thoughts. No one likes to feel ignored. As with criticism, listen openly. It's a very good sign that they are getting involved. Your pitch has been good enough to draw them in and to spark creative ideas. Nod, note down their suggestions and remember she'll quite possibly have completely forgotten everything she said the next time you meet.

YOU

Whether she asks or not, you must find an opportunity to sell yourself.

What gave you the idea?

If you haven't already used this in your introduction, here's an opportunity to talk about what inspired you.

Inspiration is what the producer wants you to provide. She can crunch the numbers – you have to be the one with vision. She wants to see how passionate you are about the project. Don't hold back. Remember, the more personal engagement, the more likely that energy will enliven the script, and the more publicity she can look forward to when the finished film is shown.

Why are you the right person for this project?

Talk about any jobs or life experiences relevant to the story. Describe the research you've uncovered, the interesting stories and characters you've met along the way, the contacts you've made.

Mention any writing experience, especially paid work, writing that's been printed or produced, competition successes, blogs written or contributed to. Remember all the things you did to build your personal CV when writing the query letter. Then you only had a few sentences. Now you have more time.

What have you made before?

Most important for documentary. Because a documentary has, by its nature, a much looser script, the producer has to ensure that the filmmaker has the ability to construct a story on the fly, deal with the unpredictable nature of reality and bring home the goods no matter what happens.

If you haven't any credits, then you need to work harder to build your credibility, expertise, writing credits, academic credentials, blog success, etc., even more than you would with a fiction pitch. You will almost certainly need to show a trailer, too (see next chapter).

What special something do you bring to everything you do? How would you describe your voice?

Again, don't wait to be asked. Seize any chance to talk about your personal approach. What ideas inspire and energise you? What stories attract you? What lights your fire – injustice, waste of talent, making people laugh? What do you love to do that you're doing here in this script?

RESPONSE 5 – I LOVE IT – SEND ME THE SCRIPT

Great. You do have the script ready to send, don't you? (Or ready within a week.)

Before you send it, make doubly sure there aren't any typos or spelling mistakes. Don't rely on your spellchecker. There are many errors it won't pick up such as words that are spelt the same but have different meanings. As with query letters, be especially careful with the most important words. I've seen scripts where the main character's name is misspelled!

Check that the script is correctly formatted, correct font, correct layout, etc. Professional film and TV scripts are laid out to very strict rules and many up-and-coming writers sabotage themselves by not looking closely enough at the format and getting an important element wrong.

You can download the full details along with a template for free from my website **www.charles-harris.co.uk** and you can also find them in my book *Teach Yourself: Complete Screenwriting Course*.

FINISHING

And then suddenly it's over. The conversation stops. Don't overstay your welcome. Whatever the outcome, finish and get out.

This is not the time to remember that other project you could have mentioned earlier. Or a key point you forgot to make about the main character. Stand up, shake hands and go. You've done the best you can.

I've seen writers talk themselves out of a deal, merely by hanging around too long. Some people won't take yes for an answer.

And if the answer is no, well, accept it and move on. Trying to fight your corner will only ruin any possible future relationship you may have with this person. And even if you have already decided you don't want a relationship with her – remember it's a small industry. She may well mention your name to other people you want to pitch to in the future.

You never know what's round the corner. There is always the next pitch… and the next.

TO SUM UP...

- Be ready with a verbal trailer and outline if asked – and keep them short.
- Use sensory language to bring the scenes to life.
- Be ready for all possible questions that may come up.
- Sell your background, inspiration and personal voice.
- When the meeting is over, it's over.

VISUALS AND **LEAVE-BEHINDS**

Should you back up your pitch with visual aids used during the meeting or printed material that you leave behind you as you finish? This very much depends – on the project and on your resources.

VISUAL AIDS

For the most part, a good pitch should need no visual back-up. Certainly not for fiction. Your job as a fiction writer is to use words to create a story and characters in the mind of the reader. Visual aids – such as trailers, artwork and photographs – will either be unnecessary or counterproductive. If your pitch is strong enough you won't need them to convince a producer to read your script. Worse, they may put him off.

Unless you are a micro-budget script, no trailer will ever be able to match the acting, lighting, art direction, editing, sound design and overall directing quality of the finished production. Yet, a producer won't be able to avoid consciously or unconsciously judging the quality of what you show, and anything less than the best professional work will count against you.

Furthermore, the pictures you create in his mind are invariably going to be far superior to anything you can afford to create.

SHORTS

If you still really want to show something – and have the resources to make a good job – then don't make a trailer: make a stand-alone short.

Aim for no longer than three minutes' running time. Make it in the same genre, using a similar milieu. Keep it contained, ideally one location, so that your money can go further, ensure the acting is good and show off your strongest storytelling skills. As with any other part of your pitch, you should get professional feedback at every stage of the process, from script to edit, and only use it if you are entirely sure it is of the highest professional quality.

The advantage of a short, as opposed to a trailer, is that it stands on its own merits. You are not saying that this is precisely what your finished movie or TV programme will look like. In addition, a short can have a valuable life of its own. A trailer has no life outside of selling a movie. A short film can be sent round the world to festivals, winning audiences – and maybe even prizes – to add to your CV.

With all visual aids, remember, you don't have to have them. So if you have the slightest doubt, don't. Focus all that energy on creating your best pitch. However, there are exceptions:

DOCUMENTARY TRAILERS

The opposite applies in documentary. Here, because there will be no detailed script to read, you need to produce a trailer to convince the producer you can deliver to a high standard.

Like a short film, a trailer for a documentary pitch should be very short. One and a half minutes is good – three minutes is an absolute maximum. It must be of broadcast quality, the best you can produce.

A good documentary trailer will be gripping and engaging. It will prove that you have access and showcase your best characters, while demonstrating the style with which you plan to make the full programme.

ANIMATION

You will also need visuals for pitching animation. The visual style of an animation is so intrinsic to its appeal that a verbal pitch will not work alone.

Print up high-quality artwork showing your main characters, primary locations, key moments of action. You may also want to create a mood board or even a sample storyboard. Anything that gives a strong feeling for your personal artistic style.

If you have access to the equipment, then a trailer or brief vignettes of key scenes would be useful. As with a documentary trailer, it goes without saying that anything you show must be of the highest standard.

MOOD BOARDS

The third exception applies if a visual is central to the story. For this you might want to bring a single blow-up picture or a more developed mood board to present.

The movie *Woman in Gold* is based on the true story of the fight by an elderly Jewish refugee to win back Gustav Klimt's celebrated painting of her aunt, stolen from her family by the Nazis. In such a case, it would be reasonable, if not essential, to bring a high-quality reproduction of the picture involved.

It might also be that you're seriously concerned that elements in the story will create an off-putting visual impression that you can't counter with words. This is more likely to apply if pitching to direct rather than write. If you feel that the people you're pitching to will be deterred by misunderstanding the look of the film, printing up images that show what you visualise could well be useful.

When director Curtis Hanson was pitching to Arnon Milchan to greenlight the 1950s-set crime movie *LA Confidential*, he and producer Michael Nathanson felt it was crucial to the pitch that Milchan understand the approach they were going for. So Hanson had a series of vintage postcards of LA blown up onto large boards, to introduce the image of prosperity. The presentation then moved on to darker pictures of scandal magazines and the actor Robert Mitchum after being jailed for drugs offences. If you watch the movie, you can see many of the images Hanson used – they became backgrounds to the opening titles.

LEAVE-BEHINDS

Leave-behinds are a different matter. It's always useful to have some material you can give the producer or agent when you shake hands at the end. At the very least, a leave-behind will ensure that the person you just met doesn't immediately forget you once you've walked out of the door. At best, it will help sell your project.

However, a word of warning. They are called leave-behinds because they come out at the end. Except for business cards, I recommend never, ever handing over material earlier in the meeting. The reason is simple: the moment you give the other person something to read, their eyes will go to the paper and not to you. You'll have lost that essential eye contact and you may struggle to get it back.

Keep that handout in your bag until the last moment.

BUSINESS CARD

A professionally printed business card is a must. Don't skimp and try to print it on your home printer. The difference will show. This is your career – after all you've invested in a computer, in the right clothes, in a phone contract, why try to save a few pounds now? Nowadays, local print shops and online services such as moo and printing.com can produce a run of professional business cards for you at very reasonable prices.

Keep the information simple. It should show your name – and a designation, such as 'Screenwriter'. You may combine this with other jobs that are relevant (such as 'Director' or 'Script Editor') but please don't add your day job if it's not in the industry. Spend the money and order a separate card.

Give your principal contact details – postal address, phone and email. You might include one social media address, such as your Twitter handle. But that's it. Some writers add a photograph, but that's really for actors and estate agents. I wouldn't.

Use one font – two at the most. This is not the time to show off your print shop's range of typefaces. Ditto with colours. I've seen writers try to make an impression by creating a card with a dozen fonts, a rainbow spectrum of colours and a quirky picture. Resist the temptation. You want to be remembered for your writing – not your card.

The size should be the standard business card size – not wide or tall or, heaven forbid, round or hexagonal – and in a reasonable weight.

And white. Why should the card be white? Because as soon as you are out of sight, the person you gave it to will turn it over and write down who you are and when you met. If you remember, in 'Making the Approach', I advised you to do the same.

ONE-SHEET OR ONE-PAGER

The other thing to leave after a pitch meeting is a one-sheet. In the film industry, the term 'one-sheet' (or 'one-pager') can have two different meanings. It can mean a treatment or synopsis in a single page (see below). Or it can mean something closer to an executive summary of your project. Here, we're talking about the summary version.

A summary one-sheet is a very valuable leave-behind as it presents the recipient with the vital information he needs to remember and, most importantly, the things you want him to say if he is to talk about your idea to a colleague.

It is divided into different areas and – as with a query letter – must fit onto a single sheet of A4 or letter-sized paper. Like a query letter, it should be printed in a simple, readable font. Divide up the paragraphs so that there is plenty of white space to entice the eye – there's nothing quite so off-putting as a sea of unbroken type.

At the top you put the title of your project and your name as the writer.

Beneath that, in pride of place, goes your strongest log line. Make sure you also say what kind of project it is – feature film, TV series, etc. You'd be surprised how many one-sheets leave you guessing. (Or, more likely, not bothering to guess but putting it straight in the bin.)

Next comes a single, short blurb. This must be in the present tense, third person and give an exciting overview of the dramatic core of your story or series. It should build on the key features of your log line – genre, protagonist, protagonist's flaw and goal. Not unlike the longer pitch discussion we talked about in the last chapter. But, unlike a full treatment (see next section), you don't need to give the ending.

You do, however, need to match your style to the genre. If a comedy, then keep the writing light and bring out the humour in your premise and in the characters. If a noir, evoke the darkness.

Two further short paragraphs should outline any important features that will help sell the story – most importantly, the world of the story, and why you are exactly the right person to be writing this.

A documentary one-sheet would also need to give an indication of the production budget and a summary of the team who will be making it. Don't put an estimated budget for a fiction one-sheet, unless you're a producer looking for finance.

Don't oversell – don't say this will be wonderfully funny, horribly scary, financially successful, etc. That's for the reader to work out.

At the bottom of your one-sheet, put your contact details. This may seem redundant but one-sheets can become detached from any other material and if you're relying on a producer keeping it with your business card you may be out of luck. What would be more tragic than if she came across your one-sheet a few weeks later, liked it, but didn't know how to find you?

Writers often ask whether to include pictures. With live-action fiction, I feel pictures look amateurish. What you're pitching is your ability with words. Your job is to create pictures in the reader's mind, using your language skills. If you can't do that, then no amount of pictures is going to help.

SUNSET OVER SARAJEVO

FEATURE FILM SCREENPLAY
BY JO BLOCKBUSTER

Conspiracy thriller. A maverick ecologist discovers an international energy corporation has been hiding unstable nuclear waste under the world's poorer cities and killed the last expert who threatened to expose them. To save his life, and the lives of millions, he must learn to trust and work with others.

The Story

When Gary Smithson begins to suspect that his employers, BEO Energy, have been risking millions of lives by secretly storing dangerous radioactive pluthocromium in city sewers, his first thought is that it must be a mistake. An idiosyncratic ecologist, who finds it difficult to get on with his fellow scientists, he becomes more fearful when his brakes fail driving from a BEO centre in the Alps. He only narrowly survives, along with his boss, Catherine Rashford.

Soon after, Rashford discovers that the last person to investigate BEO's underground facilities also died in a mysterious car crash. Gary has twenty-four hours to break into the Bosnian warehouse holding the documents that prove his case before they are destroyed. That means staying one step ahead of BEO's vicious internal security department and learning to trust Rashford, without whom he can't succeed.

Dodging BEO's men and international security services, they manage to cross Europe and finally reach Sarajevo. Here they break into the highly guarded holding facility, using all their knowledge to bypass the warehouse security systems. But as Gary retrieves the incriminating documents an unexpected alarm goes off. Under fire from the guards, they flee into the sewers deep beneath the warehouse, where the unstable nuclear waste is being stored. But is it a trap? And has the clever and ambitious Rashford betrayed him?

The World

The world of Big Energy is a cut-throat one in which companies will cut corners and take risks for a small advantage over their rivals. Governments don't dare challenge them for fear of energy price rises. The need to dispose of waste from nuclear raises the stakes even further, with incentives for too many people to turn a blind eye to the risks. A plausible company, with a strong security force ensuring no bad information leaks out, could be ready to take those risks today – at any cost.

Screenwriter Jo Blockbuster

I myself worked as an ecologist in the former Yugoslavia and have seen from the inside the dirty tricks the major energy companies get up to. I have written on the subject for local newspapers and national ecology magazines, including a number of commissioned articles on tax dodges by power companies, price fixing and cost-cutting at power stations.

The Screenplay

The completed, polished screenplay is available now, running 98 pages.

Contact details

77 Writersblock Avenue, Stockington ST31 7TM
Tel: +44 3069 990492 Mobile: +44 7700 900995
Email: jo@writeonwriting.co.uk   Web: www.writeonwriting.co.uk

SAMPLE ONE-SHEET

It's different if the visuals are an essential part of the story, as with an animation or in a film based around a key visual such as *Woman in Gold*. In such a case, you would want to include appropriate artwork – either in the text or as a cover page.

But if your picture is purely there to evoke the pictorial feel of the finished film, then it's a crutch, an attempt to hide your failure to make the words do the work. Cut the picture and improve the words.

TREATMENT

A treatment is a document that tells a shortened version of your story, and in the film and TV industry the term means exactly the same as outline, synopsis or précis. It's similar to the blurb paragraph in your summary one-sheet except that it must include the ending.

Like the summary one-sheet, a treatment should be in the present tense, third person and readable, with short paragraphs to attract the eye. A treatment can be a single page, or indeed almost any length from half a page to 15 pages or longer, depending on what's wanted.

Good treatments are not easy to write but they are very useful for producers as they allow them to get a quick overview of your story and see if you know your key story beats and whether they work. As with a pitch, you will not sell your idea on a treatment alone, so while it's important that you have a good treatment ready to send, I don't recommend volunteering to leave one unless it's been asked for. Remember, your aim should always be for the producer to ask for the script.

Of course, if he does ask for a treatment, then either hand him a printout, if you have one, or email one as soon as possible afterwards.

Treatments are also useful to you, not only to sell the script but also to help you plan it out at the early stages. You may also, as we saw earlier, be asked to send one with your initial approach. You therefore need to have a number of draft versions standing by at different lengths, ready to send.

(Like pitching, the ability to write a strong treatment is a crucial skill, though outside the scope of this book. I teach how to write powerful treatments on my blog **www.charles-harris.co.uk** and in my book *Teach Yourself: Complete Screenwriting Course*.)

SERIES PROPOSAL

If you are pitching a series, you will almost certainly be asked for a written series proposal. This is a longer document of three to six pages which begins with your summary one-sheet as an introductory page, and then takes each element and expands on it.

Thus, in the following pages you would include sections which went into more detail about your target audience, the world of the series, the writer and the central recurring characters. This would be followed by a treatment of the pilot episode plus shorter treatments and log lines for further episodes. It would normally be accompanied by the pilot script.

DOCUMENTARY PROPOSAL

Sometimes known as an **EPK** (variously Electronic Press Kit or Electronic Promo Kit). Very similar to the series proposal, your back-up material for a documentary needs to start with a summary one-sheet, giving title, length, budget, team, contact details and a brief synopsis. Unlike fiction, for a factual proposal you do want to include a striking image that will probably come from your research or a recce trip. As always, make it the best picture you have – one with iconic resonance that alone gives a compelling reason to want to watch the film.

This is followed by a half-page synopsis of the idea and then a longer treatment which expands on the key beats of the documentary as you imagine it unfolding. Use more of your striking images here to break up the text and make your proposal real, but keep the whole document to no more than four pages in all, which will then be packaged with your video trailer.

TO SUM UP...

- A good fiction pitch normally needs no visual back-up.
- Don't make a trailer for a fiction story – if necessary write and film a stand-alone short film.
- Provide slides or artwork for animation or if you think the subject demands it.
- A documentary pitch should include a short trailer.
- A summary one-sheet is a valuable leave-behind, giving the key points of your pitch.
- Have a treatment or proposal ready to give or send afterwards.

PITCHING TO A ROOM

In real life, you will make most if not all your pitches to one person. Occasionally, she may be accompanied by one or two colleagues. However, there are a few, if rare, occasions where you may want to pitch to a large audience. If this scares the living daylights out of you, don't worry. No one's going to force you to do it.

Opportunities to pitch in front of an audience usually come at festivals or competitions.

The Raindance Festival runs their 'Live Ammo' competition – for example – where a panel of industry judges selects the best pitch and awards a cash prize plus a chance to discuss your project with an industry insider. There are similar events at the London Screenwriters' Festival, Cannes and various PitchFests around the world.

Other events give you the chance to pitch to an audience which includes potential buyers, co-producers, agents and distributors.

Pitching to an audience is a little more pressurised than one-to-one, but in addition to the potential rewards it can also be great fun. And even if you don't take part, I'd advise sitting in on as many as you can, to hear how other people pitch (both well and badly) and get a sense of the other projects around.

PLANNING THE AUDIENCE PITCH

The biggest trap is time. You can't now simply say your log line and stop for questions. You need to provide a little more. However, under the pressure of nerves it's easy to start waffling on and often difficult to stop.

Find out the time limit in advance. Some pitching events set a strict 60-second rule, while others may offer as long as ten minutes. Aim to stop well before the limit, which will give you room for error and also a chance to take questions if they're allowed. It will also earn you the gratitude of the judges, who will almost certainly have had to endure far too many pitches which long outstayed their welcomes.

Start with your log line. It's your best beginning. You know now from experience that it works and it gives a tried and tested opening line. From there, you should plan out a structure that answers the key questions you'd be asked in a typical pitch meeting.

A simple and effective plan might go something like:

- Log line
- What inspired you/how this connects with you and your experience
- Main character – his strengths and flaws
- A dramatic scene that shows what he's like
- A thematic scene that illustrates the underlying dilemmas of the story
- A highly visual scene that sums it all up

As with a normal pitch, you could also open with a question or what inspired you. But beware of (a) taking too long to get to the point, and (b) getting too clever. I've sat on pitching panels and we've heard all the would-be impressive openings and cute hooks many times over. It's the meat of the idea that counts every time.

Prepare and rehearse a strong final sentence. There's nothing more soul-destroying than to find yourself dribbling to a halt. If you know your ending, then you can be confident that – however bumpy the flight – you'll find a firm landing.

The shorter the slot you've been given, the more you need to practise to ensure you can finish the pitch without rushing. You want to relax, knowing you can easily hit the right length with time to spare.

POSTURE

We focus mostly on the words we speak; however, research shows that words are only one element. Your voice and physical presence can overpower the effect of what you say. We have all seen speakers whose appearance or voice undermined them. By contrast, we've also found ourselves entranced by people who we felt from their voice and appearance were on our wavelength, who we could like and get on with.

The pressure of speaking in front of an audience can be high. The very word 'pressure' is well chosen – you can actually feel as if something is pressing down on you. Pressure also brings out all kinds of unconscious mannerisms in people, such as shifting from side to side, standing awkwardly, stepping backwards, standing with their hands in their pockets. These are all unconscious signs of the desire not to be there. But you do want to be there, or you wouldn't have stepped up. Remember – the audience is on your side. They actually want you to do well. Nobody wants to be bored; they want you to be inspiring and entertaining for your short time on stage. The producers in the audience want you to excite them with your ideas.

Make a conscious decision to relax, stand straight with your feet firmly planted and take command of the stage. Stillness is always more engaging than too much movement. Keep still, hands by your sides, head centred – and move only when you decide to move.

If you have doubts, ask a supportive friend to judge which posture looks strongest and most engaging. Some people like to practise in front of the mirror. That can be useful, although of course you won't be pitching to an image of yourself. I suggest you'll learn more by recording yourself. Video recording will help you spot mannerisms and build good habits.

One very simple and effective technique to develop when speaking is to widen your range of vision. When we are under stress, we tend to narrow our focus. It's called 'fovial vision' and is very useful if you're in the prehistoric forest running from a sabre-toothed tiger. Not so useful in pitching.

The opposite to fovial vision is 'expanded awareness'. This is a much more relaxed and resourceful state which allows you to speak and perform more effectively. You are aware of everything around you and feel calmer. Ideas and words flow more easily.

....

EXERCISE

Select something small and static on the wall facing you – preferably it should be slightly above eye level, say, a hook, a drawing pin or a small mark. Focus fully on this spot. Now – while still keeping your eyes on the spot – gradually widen your attention to become aware of the area around it. Continue to keep your eyes on the spot while you widen your awareness further, becoming aware of everything around you on both sides and indeed slightly behind.

This is expanded awareness. How does it feel? Did you feel less or more relaxed? Less or more alert?

....

VOICE

As the adrenaline flows, so our voice flattens and loses emotional range. At the same time, we automatically speak faster and higher. However, this can make your voice sound less engaging. Audiences naturally connect more strongly with voices which are lower, slower and have a wider tonal range.

No one expects you to be a consummate actor but every little helps.

....

EXERCISE

Without forcing your voice, take a few relaxed breaths and then practise speaking slightly lower and more slowly than at first might feel natural.

Now try varying the pitch, the tone, the quality of your voice – one moment thoughtful, the next horrified. One sentence can be slow and dreamily romantic – while the next vibrates with excitement. Echo your story with your voice. Voice recording can help you develop your voice, adjust any vocal tics and add vocal variety.

....

VISUAL AIDS

Some events will offer you the chance to show clips, PowerPoint slides, etc. The same rules apply as in the pitch meeting. Ask yourself if they will really help. And double-check with a professional, who you trust to tell you whether the quality is up to industry standard (both technical and content). Ask them to be brutally honest. Better to know now than when it's too late.

If you must use PowerPoint slides, keep them short, very short. Slides are for bullet points – not whole paragraphs. No more than two to three words per bullet point and one to three bullet points per slide. And very few slides overall. By all means, brighten them up with relevant and professional pictures. And did I say keep them short?

If using any back-up materials of any kind, dress-rehearse using them. If slides, do you know precisely where they fit? If they're physical prints or artwork cards, how much time do you need to bring them out? You don't want to spend precious seconds fumbling with a folder. And are they big enough to be seen at the back?

Make a checklist of what you need to bring with you – I guarantee if you try to rely on memory you'll forget something vital on the day.

THINGS *NOT* TO WORRY ABOUT

Ums and errs... A small amount of hesitancy is natural, and trying to eradicate all vocal tics might make you more self-conscious. Ditto with repeated words or phrases. However, if you find you frequently fall into particular verbal mannerisms, slow down. Give yourself time to speak more clearly and with greater control. It will pay dividends. Slow is good. It draws listeners in.

Pauses... People sometimes think they have to keep going no matter what. It's okay to stop and think of the right word, from time to time. In fact, the effort of trying to find... precisely... the best word... to say... can often be captivating.

Not being perfect... You aren't perfect. Nor is Leonardo DiCaprio or Dame Judi Dench. You're not there to be perfect. You are there because you have a great idea and you want other people to share in it. In the end, it's the idea that counts. All the rest is just window dressing.

ON THE DAY

Try to arrive at the venue well in advance. If possible, stand where you'll be pitching from and get a feel for the place. It all helps you feel more in control. If you have technical requirements, speak to the appropriate people, load up slides and clips, etc., and make sure they all work.

Find out about sound and lighting. Will you be holding a mic or will they pin one to your lapel? How do you cue slides or clips? Will you be able to see the audience or will you have lights in your eyes and be able to see nothing at all? Strong lighting can be off-putting at first, but you'll soon get used to it.

Talking to an audience can feel intimidating if you've not done it before. Remember, they want you to be good. Be professional and do your stuff. Don't prepare special jokes. If humour arises naturally from the pitch, that's great, but don't wait for the laughs. Audiences are unpredictable. Keep focused on your pitch.

Include the whole audience in your presentation. Get into expanded awareness and favour different areas from time to time. If you find it distracting to make eye contact with people watching you, then here's a useful trick: don't look at individuals, look at the gaps between them. The effect is the same; everyone assumes you are looking at someone, but not them.

Be aware of the danger of mind-reading the crowd. Some years ago, while I was running a workshop, I noticed a man sitting at the back, arms folded over his chest, looking like thunder. Clearly, I decided, I'd said something to offend him, but I couldn't work out what it might have been. At the first break, I went up to him and asked if everything was all right.

Yes, he said. But he found the workshop so interesting that he was trying hard to remember every detail. It turned out that this was simply how he looked when he was concentrating.

So don't jump to conclusions. People can yawn because they've been working long hours. People can get distracted because of problems at home. Not every reaction is down to you.

NODDERS AND SMILERS

One of the most valuable tips I was ever given was to look for **nodders and smilers**. In most large audiences, you'll find a few people who simply like to nod and/or smile from the start. Locate where these nodders and smilers are sitting and use them as your supporters. Address much of what you say to them. They'll make you feel good. You might even feel like nodding and smiling in turn.

TO SUM UP...

- Know how long you have and plan to be shorter.
- Start with your log line.
- Plan to answer the same key questions as at a pitch meeting.
- A positive posture and voice are as important as the words you use.
- The shorter the slot, the more you need to practise in advance.
- Arrive early to check out the venue.
- Find the nodders and smilers.

WHEN THINGS GO **WRONG**

If you pitch for long enough, everything that can go wrong will go wrong. Producers will cancel and postpone. Or take phone calls all through the meeting. Fire alarms will go off. Technology won't work. Whatever has been told to you in advance will turn out to be different. Your five-minute slot will suddenly become one minute. Your clips will be without sound...

In my time, I've turned up for events where there were supposed to be 140 people and because of a bureaucratic mistake there were only three. And I've turned up expecting three and found 140. I've gone to pitch meetings with a co-producer only to see him suddenly struck down by illness. I once had to do a presentation that relied crucially on five film clips but couldn't show them because someone had mislaid a crucial cable. So I worked out a way to describe the clips as I went along.

Sometimes the problems come from inside – you lose faith in yourself, procrastinate, feel lacking in confidence or find yourself making elementary mistakes.

To pitch well takes three things: you need to have the skills to create a good pitch in the first place, you need to have the right strategies to know who to pitch to and when – and you need the psychological skills that I call the **Mental Game**.

In this chapter we look at your Mental Game and how to win it.

OUTSIDE YOUR COMFORT ZONE

When you set out to pitch, there will be challenges. You will fail to achieve some goals. You will get rejected. You are moving outside your comfort zone. Remember the chapter on the Inner Story. Just as your characters have an inner story, so do you. You, too, have to overcome your flaws if you are to achieve your happy ending. And like them you will find the world constantly challenging you to prove how much you have progressed.

The German poet and playwright Goethe said, 'The moment you definitely commit yourself, then Providence moves too. All sorts of things occur to help you that would never otherwise have occurred.' And it is true.

It is also true that Providence moves to try and stop you! It's as if the universe wants to test just how committed you really are.

PROBLEMS IN MAKING THE APPROACH

PROCRASTINATION

We all have those times when we want to hide under the duvet, or play Angry Birds, rather than work on our writing, pick up the phone or email a producer we'd like to meet.

A common reason for procrastination is that we are afraid of rejection. Disliking rejection is natural. However, the writer who never got rejected never sent anything out. Rejection is a part of the writer's life. Every writer, however great and successful, has had work turned down. The question is what they did about it.

The playwright John Osborne revolutionised theatre in the 1950s with his play *Look Back in Anger*. It smashed through the cosy, middle-class dramas that were the vogue and brought new characters and stories to the stage – going on to be produced all over the world. It was initially rejected by almost every theatre in Britain... including the Royal Court, the theatre that finally staged it.

Playwrights, poets, novelists, and of course screenwriters, have all been rejected many times before they succeed.

Rejection doesn't mean you're bad. It means you were brave enough to finish a script and brave enough to make an approach to a possible buyer. Maybe the timing was wrong. Maybe you need to make adjustments to your pitch. Either way, unlike the majority of wannabe writers, you didn't sit on your backside, you took a risk.

You did. You stepped out of your comfort zone. A rejection, looked at this way, is something to be proud of. A new battle scar to add to the list.

VALUES

When writers tell me they've lost heart in a project, I always take them back to the inner story – the project's inner story and their own. Every single story you see on screen, good and bad, has had to deal with a thousand problems to reach its audience. What keeps the writers going, as with their characters, is the inner journey. What are you trying to achieve? What lights your fire? What are your values? What's important to you?

This is why I asked you about your own values so early in this book. The clearer you are about your own reasons and values, the stronger will become your desire to do the work and overcome the many obstacles that stand in your way. Ask yourself what you'll gain from achieving your goal. And how achieving that goal will affect others: people you know, people you don't yet know, maybe even people you may never know.

The truth is that to go beyond your comfort zone is risky. Risks are risky. There are no guarantees. You can fail. But if you focus on your values, the goals that are important to your life, you can decide which is more important – staying safe or taking a risk on success.

EXERCISE

Go back to the exercise you did in the second chapter and look again at the reasons you gave for wanting to sell this script. Remind yourself of the values you set out there. Your own motivations. Maybe add a few more.

Is this story one that needs to be told? Or one that will give enjoyment? Will selling this script help build your career so you can do more to bring your vision to future audiences? If money is your aim, what will that money enable you to do? Or enable others to do – your family, friends or causes you support?

SECONDARY GAIN

Rejection is not the only reason that stops people. Many people are equally afraid of success. Success can bring its own problems. Perhaps you're afraid of being resented by other, less successful, writers. Or scared you can't write a second script as well as the first. Reluctant to outshine someone who is close to you. Or anxious that you'll find yourself losing touch with your friends or family. Sometimes it's safer to avoid all those issues by not trying in the first place.

In the psychological studies of NLP (Neuro-Linguistic Programming) this is called **Secondary Gain**. Something you are gaining by *not* doing what you really want to do.

If you find that avoiding doing what you want is bringing you secondary gains, then you have a choice. You can decide to continue not doing it and choose a different goal. Or you can negotiate with yourself. You can seek out a better way of achieving the same gain.

I was once pitching a film I very much wanted to direct, a story which took place mostly at night, in the middle of winter. The pitch was strong, but somehow I knew I wasn't selling it as well as I knew I could.

One day I stopped to work out what was going wrong and realised I had much to gain from not selling the script. I'd calculated I'd need ten weeks filming, mostly all-night shoots, exterior, in the cold, away from home. By not pitching successfully, I was avoiding all that.

Once I understood this, I realised I could make changes. For example, I found ways to shoot most of the exteriors indoors by day, in the warm, by building an exterior set in a studio. I reduced the schedule to spend less time away and arranged more opportunities to get home during breaks in filming. I made a deal with myself that I'd only go ahead with the project on terms that worked for me. And once I did that, the pitching improved.

....

EXERCISE

If you are avoiding doing something you know you want to do – ask yourself if there is something you're gaining by not doing it.

Make a list of all the possible secondary gains that come from not doing what you want to do.

Now work out how you might satisfy those needs in other ways. Ways which would allow you to achieve your goal.

....

SETTING GOALS

Most of us set vague, imprecise goals and then find to our surprise that we don't achieve them. The more precise your goals, the more likely it is you'll make them happen. 'Selling your script' is too vague. 'Sending out one query letter a week' is far more likely to be achieved.

Next, make your goals realistic and relative to your experience. Better to set yourself a goal you can reach, and feel good by reaching it, than set a goal that's too hard. If you've never pitched before, then pitching to two or three friends could be a realistic goal.

Aim a little low to build your confidence. If you set a goal to pitch to eight friends and only pitch to four, you feel a failure. Whereas if you set a goal to pitch to two and end up pitching to four, you feel a success – same result, completely different feeling.

Once you've reached that goal, you need more of a stretch. Maybe getting a review of your pitch from a feedback service. Or approaching one industry professional.

Once you've set your realistic goal, write it down. You might want to keep a list of all your goals. Make them specific and date them – that is, don't say, I'm going to approach 'some' agents 'in a few weeks'. Say, 'I'm going to approach one agent in the week starting 4 May.'

Visualise what it looks like to achieve that goal. Think about all the things you'll have done to achieve it. And all the things you'll be able to do as a result afterwards. Then share the goal with a trusted friend – someone you can trust to support you but also hold you to account.

PROBLEMS IN PREPARING TO PITCH

CONFIDENCE

The quickest and easiest way to become confident is knowing you've created a good pitch. Which is why I lay so much stress on creating the pitch in this book. There's a sureness that comes when you know your idea has that magic spark.

The next step is to have the experience of pitching that pitch, and receiving positive responses. Start with friends and family and build on that. Build confidence simply by going out and doing it, time and time again.

ACT AS IF

It's a strange fact, but you can act yourself into changing your emotional state. If you act as if you're nervous, then your unconscious mind will believe it and start to feel more nervous. By contrast, if you act as if you're confident, it will begin to reward you with the confidence you were pretending to have.

NERVES ARE ENERGY

When I'm not writing or making films, I practise a martial art: Aikido. One thing I learned very early in my Aikido training is that people are apt to confuse their feelings. When a stressful situation arises, such as being attacked, our bodies get ready to do something about it. To do this it produces large amounts of adrenaline. This prepares our muscles to work efficiently – to run away or to fight. As it flows round the body, we grow tense yet energised; we may find ourselves feeling cold. Our hands may even shake slightly, as the muscles rev up ready for action.

However, if you're not careful you might mistake these inner changes for signs of fear. Feeling afraid then makes you feel more afraid, which in turn creates more adrenaline, in a vicious circle.

The important thing to realise is that those first signs aren't anything to worry about. Quite the reverse. That adrenaline is necessary for your body and mind to work well.

When you approach someone important at a networking event, say, or walk into a pitch meeting, the adrenaline will flow. Welcome it. You need to be focused – and the adrenaline will help you perform at your peak of efficiency.

Take a deep breath. Relax. Think of what we call nerves as useful energy. The energy you need to do your job well.

....

EXERCISE

One very powerful way to approach a meeting is to visualise it in three steps.

Find a quiet place, where you know you can stay undisturbed. Turn off any phones or other devices. Make yourself comfortable and relax.

Now, bring to mind someone who is expert at pitching. It might be someone you know personally or a successful writer or filmmaker you admire. Close your eyes and imagine this person going into that pitch meeting. Use all your senses to make the scene as vivid as you can. Notice all the details: the way the room looks as they walk in, the person or people they're meeting, the clothes they wear. Hear what they say, as if you have a high-quality recording. And feel what the expert feels, as they go through the meeting. How they turn their nerves into focused energy.

Now fade out the picture and fade in at the start again, except the second time this expert at pitching is wearing your face! It's still them, with all their experience and confidence, but they look like you. As before, see them walk in, hear what is said and feel what they feel, the pitching expert with your face.

Fade out and fade in again for the third run. This time, the person is you. You're looking through your own eyes, with all you've learned from watching your chosen mentor. Start at the beginning and see what you see as you walk into the room yourself. Hear what is said to you and what you say in return. And feel what you feel in yourself as you take the meeting: asking questions, listening, establishing a strong rapport with the person in the room.

At the end, fade out for a moment, stop and think. Is that how you'd like the meeting to be? Can you imagine actually having the meeting go the way you've foreseen it? How would you feel if it did?

....

PROBLEMS IN THE MEETING ITSELF

Pitching is a roller-coaster. One minute you're up, then you're down, then you're back up again. Whatever can happen will happen – go with the flow and accept it with good grace.

Screenwriter Shelley Katz says, 'I had a two-thirty meeting with a corpulent, famous US producer. He came in all jolly and rosy-cheeked and I gave it my all. He didn't stop me with any of the usual "We have a movie about lawyers or doctors or whatever". I thought it was going great. Until I heard the loud snore. Moral: try and avoid meetings just after lunch.'

If disaster strikes, stay cool and professional. Remember, the next pitch is just the next pitch. You're in this for the long term, not just one meeting.

NOT BEING AWARE OF WHO YOU'RE TALKING TO

A screenwriter told me about working with a famous comic who had an idea for a show.

'We met and created the pitch, about a single guy, living his life. Sounds weak, but remember the star was going to be a very famous comic. We make a meeting and go in. Because of his status we get the entire network development staff sitting in on it. Seven people, men and women. So he makes the pitch. And it is one of the funniest pitches I've ever heard. The laughs never stopped.

'The network honcho says: WE SOLD IT IN THE ROOM!!! A rarity, but sometimes dreams come true.

'Two days later they passed. We were stunned. Then I remembered one part of his pitch where his character is expecting a visit from a hot neighbour woman. All excited, he opens the door, finding to his dismay that it's not her but, in his words, "the fat chick!" At the time I remember looking over at the overweight female executive sitting at the end of the table, not laughing. That was the end of that.'

Be aware of who you're talking to. What you consider to be a trivial joke may be deeply personal to them.

SELF-CRITICISING

More than your idea, you are selling your own confidence in your idea. By all means, be flexible and open to suggestion, but don't fall apart at the first criticism. One screenwriter remembered an instance in Hollywood.

'My agent, a producer and I went to a network to pitch a show based on the life of a drug dealer, who, while spending ten years in federal prison, became an expert jail house lawyer. After getting out he landed himself a job at a law firm where he used his intimate knowledge of prison and the law to help the lawyers he worked for find unique solutions. We met with him several times and worked out a pitch, which we all agreed on.

'So we all go to the meeting, including the man whose life it was. An amateur in showbiz, by the way. I make the pitch. They're very interested. I mean, very. So they ask questions. Locale? Other characters? Et cetera.

'Then the buyer has a suggestion contrary to what I pitched, that we'd considered and dismissed. Before I could tell her what a great idea she had (gotta do that with buyers) the guy jumps in and says – "Thank you! I've been telling these guys it should be that way but they don't listen to me!" The meeting ended a few seconds later.

'In the elevator he said he thought it went well. I said, "No, it didn't, and in fact, after you displayed the lack of cohesion in our group, they will pass." Which they did. And we dropped the guy's story. The lesson? Never disagree with your partners in front of a buyer.'

The same applies even if you're on your own. There's a fine line between accepting suggestions and criticising yourself. Under pressure, it's all too easy to assume the other person can see all your faults and try to dive in and pre-empt them with self-criticism.

If you find yourself doing that, stop. There's an important distinction between praising their ideas and criticising your own. If you've done the preparation and had good feedback, you can afford to listen to suggestions with confidence and a professional attitude.

LACK OF RAPPORT

When you meet possible producers and agents, you want to establish a working rapport. Most often, if you've prepared properly, you will do this. But sometimes there's no rapport at all. Or it disappears at some point. There may be a number of reasons for this. Something may have happened to distract the other person – an interruption, a phone call or even just a new thought. They could be in a bad mood, following an earlier problem that is nothing to do with you. Some people even like to be deliberately cold and offhand to see how the writer responds. This may not be conscious. There are producers who feel it's their job to make your job as difficult as possible, as a challenge.

Whatever the reason, you have to deal with it.

What you'll probably do at first is blame yourself. But understand that, if the producer is distant and detached, it's almost certainly nothing to do with you. If they don't want to build a rapport with you, that's their choice.

If they're cool, accept that's the style they like and be (politely) cool yourself. Remain professional and be detached too.

Ironically, what you're doing by following their lead actually puts you in a kind of rapport with them. By adopting their own coolness, you are keeping in step. And very often you'll notice the other person start to relax and warm up.

TO SUM UP...

- Dealing with problems means raising your Mental Game.
- Rejection doesn't mean you're bad – it means you've taken the risk.
- Remember your reasons for writing in the first place.
- Deal with any possible secondary gain.
- Nerves are really just useful energy.
- Pitching is a roller-coaster – go with the flow.

FOLLOW UP

And then...

And then there's that time when it all works. For a few glorious minutes, it all falls into place. All the hard work has been worthwhile. Every word you say is a gem. They love your ideas. They can't wait to read your scripts.

The people who've never had any problems never appreciate their successes either. For all the problems and disasters, when you finally succeed, it tastes so much sweeter.

You feel ten feet tall. The sun shines. The birds sing. For a few moments all is right with the world. You've pitched. To one person or to 200.

WHAT NEXT?

It's said that the most beautiful words in any language are your own name. To which I would add that the second most beautiful words are *thank* and *you*. So, the first thing you do after you've pitched is send an email:

- If he turned you down, thank him for taking the time to meet you. If he asked to see the treatment or script, thank him and send what he requested.

File his business card. Make a note of what was said in your contacts spreadsheet as soon as possible, before your memory fades. If appropriate, you may want to use what you've learned immediately, adjusting the pitch for next time, maybe even making necessary changes to the treatment and/or script. And get on with making your next approach and writing your next script.

HOW LONG DO YOU GIVE THEM TO REPLY?

If a producer doesn't acknowledge receipt of a treatment or screenplay within a week, I'll phone to confirm it hasn't gone astray. Emails can get lost, although it's more likely he just can't be bothered to tell you it arrived.

Once you know he's received the script, give him about a month to get back to you. If you've heard nothing in that time, you should ask how things are going and when you might expect to hear.

He may answer – or he may not. Everyone is different. Some companies turn scripts around very quickly and efficiently; others can take six months. Some may never say anything at all.

Because of this, you have every right to continue pitching. Unless he's asked for an exclusive look, he can't expect you to wait for weeks or months without trying elsewhere. If he has asked to read it exclusively – that's a great response. But make sure you're clear about how long a period you're giving him. He should agree to come back to you in a very short time – a week or so, I'd say – after which you are free to tout it around again.

THEN GET OUT THERE PITCHING AGAIN

Keep improving your log lines, trying them on your friends, getting feedback and approaching producers and agents, one by one, until it becomes a habit. Soon you'll be pitching week in week out – to yourself and others. Pitching will have become an integral part of your work and your life.

It will be the way you judge whether your projects are worth developing. It will be the tool you use to see if your scripts are on the right track. It will be a natural part of your ability to sell your work.

You'll be pitching as a professional.

TO SUM UP...

- Sometimes it all goes well.
- Say thank you.
- If necessary, confirm any material has been received.
- Get pitching again.
- Make pitching a natural part of your work as a professional.

RESOURCES

SUGGESTED READING

You need a good vocabulary for pitching – which doesn't mean you need long, clever words – rather a good variety of short ones that are precisely right for the job. The best way to build that vocabulary is reading.

As a minimum, you should keep a **dictionary** and **thesaurus** – you can find good versions online and in word processors; however, I believe there's still something special about having physical copies next to your desk. A **reverse dictionary** is also an invaluable aid, if you're struggling for the right way to express a thought. As the name suggests, instead of looking up a word to find its definition, you look up the definition to find the word.

Read all the pitches you can find. People ask me where they can find pitches. They're everywhere. In film and TV reviews, blurbs in the listings magazines, when you press the '*i*' button on the TV remote, in trade magazines, on websites, anywhere anyone talks about stories on screen.

You should also be reading as many screenplays as possible – you can find thousands online for free and you can also buy them as books or as the original scripts. A wide diet of other reading matter is also essential: novels, non-fiction, plays, poetry. Poetry can be particularly useful as poets have to fit their information into a small space and yet still ensure it packs a strong emotional punch.

FOR FURTHER STUDY

Much of the material in this book builds on the ideas on pitching in my book *Teach Yourself: Complete Screenwriting Course* (John Murray Learning, 2014). This takes you through the entire process of developing a script or series for cinema or TV. You'll recognise some of the key concepts and also meet new techniques and skills that you'll need for creating the initial ideas, writing treatments, and writing and editing the script itself.

If you want to develop your screenwriting, you can never read enough books on it. Every book has a nugget of information or more or can inspire you to new heights. Here are a few of my favourites, some of which I've referred to in the text:

- *The 21st Century Screenplay* – Linda Aronson (Allen & Unwin, 2010; Silman James, 2011). This highly insightful guide to how a screenplay works begins with the basics and then accelerates into a detailed analysis of the many variables of different narrative structures.

- *Alternative Scriptwriting: Beyond the Hollywood Formula* – Ken Dancyger and Jeff Rush (Focal Press, 2013). One of the few books that deals with breaking the rules, it also offers rare but welcome coverage of genre.

- *The Devil's Guide to Hollywood* – Joe Eszterhas (Gerald Duckworth & Co., 2007). Much wise (and worldly-wise) advice from one who's entered the Devil's lair and told the tale.

- *How to Make Money Scriptwriting* – Julian Friedmann (Intellect Books, 2000). An agent's no-nonsense view of the industry and what it takes to survive and succeed.

- *Inside Story* – Dara Marks (Three Mountain Press, 2007). Insightful analysis of how character journey connects with the outer story.

- *Raindance Writers' Lab: Write and Sell the Hot Screenplay* – Elliot Grove (Focal Press, 2008). Direct and accessible, from the creator of the Raindance Film Festival.

- *Save the Cat* – Blake Snyder (Michael Wiese Productions, 2005). A favourite from the moment it came out. The Hollywood system made simple.

- *Selling Your Story in 60 Seconds* – Michael Hauge (Michael Wiese Productions, 2006). Clear and practical advice on preparing the pitch and using it in action.

- *Writers' & Artists' Yearbook* – (A&C Black, annually). Reference work for TV and film companies, agents, publishers and magazines, together with useful advice sections.

INDUSTRY DIRECTORIES, PRINT AND ONLINE

- Kays – **www.kays.co.uk**
- KFTV – **www.kftv.com**
- The Knowledge – **www.theknowledgeonline.com**
- Mandy – **www.mandy.com**

TRADES

- *Hollywood Reporter* – Cinema and TV: **www.hollywoodreporter.com**
- *Screen International* – Cinema, UK-based, global coverage: **www.screeninternational.com**
- *Variety* – Cinema and TV, US-based: **www.variety.com**
- *Broadcast* – UK TV and radio: **www.broadcastnow.co.uk/Broadcast**
- *Televisual* – UK TV, radio and video: **www.televisual.com**

OTHER USEFUL WEBSITES

- BBC Writers Room – **www.bbc.co.uk/writersroom** – Strong resource for new writers looking to write for the BBC (or anyone else).

- BFI – **www.bfi.org.uk** – British Film Institute, provides funds to support screenwriters and filmmakers as well as other educational resources, films to watch online and in the BFI's own cinemas.

- Cinando – **www.cinando.com** – Database of industry people, facts and figures, including festival delegates. Subscription based.

- Drew's Script-O-Rama – **www.script-o-rama.com** – One of the largest sources of free screenplays and treatments to read. Mostly cinema but some TV.

- Euroscript – **www.euroscript.co.uk** – Originally London Screenwriters' Workshop, the first screenwriters' workshop in the world. Free networking events, screenwriting competitions, seminars, industry news and articles on many aspects of screenwriting.

- The Internet Movie Database – **www.imdb.com** – Largest database for cinema and TV. Invest in the IMDb Pro version for fuller contact info on companies, producers, directors and cast.

- Raindance – **www.raindance.org** – The biggest indie film festival in the world; also runs workshops for filmmakers internationally.

- Shooting People – **www.shootingpeople.org** – Discussion lists for screenwriters and filmmakers, with news of events and courses, low-budget work opportunities and a pitching forum where you post your pitches to the community.

- Simply Scripts – **www.simplyscripts.com** – Hundreds of downloadable scripts and treatments, including many of the most recent Oscar-nominated screenplays.

FURTHER CONTACT

If you liked this book, you can find me at **www.charles-harris.co.uk** – my website and blog, with articles, hints and tips on screenwriting, book reviews, novels, crime and useful templates you can download. Here you'll also be able to join my mailing list for the latest information on pitching, workshops, free events and industry gossip.

Feel free to contact me and share your experiences and successes, ask questions and suggest further subjects to cover in my blog. Or just to say hi.

You can also follow me on Twitter at **@chasharris,**
on Facebook at **www.facebook.com/charlesharris008**
and on LinkedIn at **uk.linkedin.com/in/charlesharris01**

INDEX

About Us

In addition to Creative Essentials, Oldcastle Books has a number of other imprints, including No Exit Press, Kamera Books, Pulp! The Classics, Pocket Essentials and High Stakes Publishing **> oldcastlebooks.co.uk**

Checkout the kamera film salon for independent, arthouse and world cinema **> kamera.co.uk**

For more information, media enquiries and review copies please contact Clare **> marketing@oldcastlebooks.com**